THE BEATITUDES

A JOURNEY HOME

TOM KINGERY

WESTBOW
PRESS®
A DIVISION OF THOMAS NELSON
& ZONDERVAN

WestBow Press books may be ordered through booksellers or by contacting:

WestBow Press
A Division of Thomas Nelson & Zondervan
1663 Liberty Drive
Bloomington, IN 47403
www.westbowpress.com
844-714-3454

ISBN: 979-8-3850-0252-8 (sc)
ISBN: 979-8-3850-0254-2 (e)

Library of Congress Control Number: 2023913022

Print information available on the last page.

WestBow Press rev. date: 07/13/2023

CONTENTS

INTRODUCTION

Then Jesus said,
"There was a man who had two sons.
The younger of them said to his father,
'Father, give me the share of the property that will belong to me.'
So he divided his property between them.
A few days later the younger son gathered all he had
and traveled to a distant country,
and there he squandered his property in dissolute living.
When he had spent everything,
a severe famine took place throughout that country,
and he began to be in need.
So he went and hired himself out to one of the citizens of that country,
who sent him to his fields to feed the pigs.
He would gladly have filled himself with the
pods that the pigs were eating;
and no one gave him anything.
But when he came to himself he said,
'How many of my father's hired hands have bread enough and to spare,
but here I am dying of hunger!
I will get up and go to my father, and I will say to him,
"Father, I have sinned against heaven and before you;
I am no longer worthy to be called your son;
treat me like one of your hired hands." '
So he set off and went to his father.
But while he was still far off, his father saw him
and was filled with compassion;
he ran and put his arms around him and kissed him.

Then the son said to him,
'Father, I have sinned against heaven and before you;
I am no longer worthy to be called your son.'
But the father said to his slaves,
'Quickly, bring out a robe—the best one—and put it on him;
put a ring on his finger and sandals on his feet.
And get the fatted calf and kill it,
and let us eat and celebrate;
for this son of mine was dead and is alive again;
he was lost and is found!'
And they began to celebrate.
Luke 15:11-24

You are the prodigal one. You've hit bottom -- hard. it wasn't sudden, but you've lost everything. All you can think now is that you don't want to be – Here –. Over and over you replay the foolishness that led you down this road. You wish you never made all the mistakes you made.

You can't go back, can you? You wish you could, but it just doesn't seem possible. You left. Were you bored? Did you want some excitement? You wanted to do something new, even risky. Well, now you're here. Your plans fell apart. You fell apart. You can't undo the past; and you don't have much of a future. What can you do? Where can you go?

Home!

The Beatitudes are a journey – a journey home. The scenery is not that pleasant… at first. But the thought of "Home" beats a blessed rhythm with each step in that direction. Tears well up when you think about what you left so long ago. There were so many blessings at home. Can you feel blessed again? Not yet, and, yes!

Examine the Beatitudes with me. Blessings are there, but they create a new future. "Blessed are…" and "They shall be…" Life is a journey. Grace is a journey. Feeling blessed propels us forward. But how do we know we are blessed? By the awareness of home; by the desire to arrive; and sometimes by looking back. Your thoughts of home are a backward look; but because that's where you're going, it is, now, more of a forward idea. When you look back at where you don't want to be anymore – Here – it doesn't really bring much of a sense of blessing. But you just won't be "here" any longer.

You're going home.

Blessed

You are already blessed. You don't need faith to know it. Can your eyes see? Can your ears hear? Count the blessings. We are made in such a way that life is awesome. Even before we know God, even without God we are blessed! Can you swallow? Even if you can't, any one of our other senses is amazing!

Cover one eye. You can still see, because you have another! Often it is when we lose our vision that we realize how blessed we were to have been able to see. The same goes for all our senses.

Can you breathe? Can you walk? Even when it's hard to do so, we are still blessed. What about hearing the sound of a baby cooing... the scent of baby powder, baby oil, baby diapers (!) all are gifts by which we have been blessed.

Don't take anything for granted. be grateful for all you have going for you and all you can do.

What have you seen in this glorious world? Have you watched a sunrise or a sunset? Have you smelled the rain on a hot summer day? Have you felt the breeze? Wow! I could go on forever.

There are thousands of blessings we can experience. Blessings abound when you look for them. Start counting blessings and you cease to feel needy!

The Beatitudes are more than Jesus telling His hearers the positive thought that they are blessed, and, that they can be blessed in the future. They are stages in a journey – a journey home. In a way, they seem incomplete, because the journey isn't finished with the last Beatitude in the Gospel of Matthew. But they help us understand the steps we need to take to get home. Each chapter will dig into what Christ has said when He told us we are blessed.

The good news is that we ARE blessed! Let's catch the blessing!

SCRIPTURES

To inspire a further consideration of an understanding of blessedness, here are several relevant passages of Scripture:

Genesis 12:3 – I will bless those who bless you, and the one who curses you I will curse; and in you all the families of the Earth shall be blessed .

Numbers 6:24-26 – The Lord bless you and keep you; the Lord make his face to shine upon you, and be gracious to you; the Lord lift up his countenance upon you, and give you peace

Deuteronomy 28:2-6 – All these blessings shall come upon you and overtake you, if you obey the Lord your God: Blessed shall you be in the city, and blessed shall you be in the field. Blessed shall be the fruit of your womb, the fruit of your ground and the fruit of your livestock, both the increase of your cattle and the issue of your flock. Blessed shall be your basket and your kneading bowl. Blessed shall you be when you come in, and blessed shall you be when you go out .

Psalm 33:12 – Happy is the nation whose God is the Lord. the people who he has chosen as his heritage.

Psalm 34:8 – Oh taste and see that the Lord is good; happy are those who take refuge in him

Psalm 103:1-2 – Bless the Lord, O my soul, and all that is within me bless His holy name. Bless the Lord, O my soul, and do not forget all his benefits.

Psalm 112:1-2 – Praise the Lord! Happy are those who fear the Lord, who greatly delight in his commandments. Their descendants will be mighty in the land; the generation of the upright will be blessed.

Psalm 118:26 – Blessed is the one who comes in the name of the Lord. We bless you from the house of the Lord.

Proverbs 22:9 – Those who are generous are blessed, for they share their bread with the poor .

Jeremiah 17:7 – Blessed are those who trust in the Lord, whose trust is in the Lord .

Luke 11:28 – But he said, "Blessed rather are those who hear the word of God and obey it."

Ephesians 1:3 – Blessed be the God and father of our Lord Jesus Christ, who has blessed us in Christ with every spiritual blessing in the Heavenly places .

James 1:12 – Blessed is anyone who endures temptation. Such a one has stood the test and will receive the crown of life that the Lord has promised to those who love him .

James 1:25 – But those who look into the perfect law, the law of liberty, and persevere, being not hearers who forget but doers who act – they will be blessed in their doing .

1 Peter 3:14-15a – But even if you do suffer for doing what is right, you are blessed. Do not fear what they fear, and do not be intimidated, but in your heart sanctify Christ as Lord .

Revelation 5:12 – Worthy is the lamb that was slaughtered to receive power and wealth and wisdom in might and honor and glory and blessing!

WHAT TO DO

Read the story of the Prodigal son (Luke 15:11-32) several times. Put yourself in the story. How have you been like the prodigal son? How have you been like the father? How have you been like the older brother? How have you been like the enablers for the prodigal?

Think of what "home" might be for you. Can you go back there? How would it feel?

Consider your own journey. Are you where you thought you would be? What directional changes have you made? Why?

Think about some of the ways you are blessed.

Consider some of the ways you can be a blessing.

What does "forward" mean for you? Where would you like to go?

Consider what it might mean to "start over". Have you ever had to do so?

A PRAYER

Almighty God, I am not worthy of all the blessings I have received. But You are worthy. You are so gracious to lavish so much upon me, I am thankful. I have eyes that see and ears that hear; I have a sense of smell and a sense of touch; I can also taste and know that life is good. With my mind I can count my blessings and rejoice. With my heart I can love and proclaim Your will. Please, surround me with Your blessings and I will rejoice in all You are giving me. In Jesus's name I pray. Amen.

A POEM

You Can't Go Back
You can't go back. You're different now.
You remember the way, but you don't know how
To make the change you know you must
And find a friend that you can trust.
Your foolishness still plays a part
In how you've broken your own heart..
What really matters is that you know
That there's a place that you might go
Where someone just might welcome you
And see beyond what you can't do.
You hope for mercy; you dream of times
When every hill had easy climbs.
Now, every step you take might bring
You closer to some higher thing.
You're on your way. You want to say
That there can be a better day.

CHAPTER ONE

THE POOR IN SPIRIT

Blessed are the poor in spirit,
for theirs is the kingdom of heaven.
Matthew 5:3

<u>The Beatitudes</u> – If the Beatitudes are seven in number, seven is a symbol of divine completeness. If they are eight, as most assume, they form a heavenly octive of harmony in the song of the Kingdom of God. If they are 10, as some scholars try to suggest was Matthew's intention (because he does proclaim Jesus as the new Moses the new deliverer bringing a new law from a new Sinai, through The Sermon on the Mount), they are a new decalog, a new 10 Commandments.

Here, Jesus is outlining the living law of the New Kingdom. He proclaims, here, the character of the Christian Life. He has seen the so-called righteousness of his day and takes issue with it. Through his proclamation of the Beatitudes he is throwing down a gauntlet before the world's accepted standards. Jesus had a tendency to turn things upside down. Where the world seems to say that riches are a blessing, for example, Jesus turns and seems to announce the very opposite.

The Beatitudes come into clearer focus, however, when they are set against their legitimate opposites. The opposite of being poor in spirit is being proud in spirit; the opposite of those who mourn is those who are frivolous and carefree; the opposite of the meek is the aggressive; the opposite of those who hunger and thirst for righteousness is those who are indifferent or apathetic; the opposite of the merciful is the vengeful; the opposite of the pure in heart is the perverted in heart; the opposite of peacemakers is the warmongers; and the opposite of the persecuted is the compromisers, those who always play it safe.

The Beattitudes may take on a fuller meaning as they are set against their opposites, but the most amazing thing the Beattitudes seem to be doing is stating who is blessed in the eyes of God!

Blessing – The meaning of blessedness in the Beatitudes is a divine sort of happiness, the highest kind of joy, a sort of incomparable bliss and ecstasy that fills the heart so full it's bearers are able to say "my cup runneth over." Jesus proclaims this almost transcendental state of being as a present endowment of the down-and-out, the voiceless, and the peaceful; and it would seem obvious to any religion of, the righteous and the faithful.

But everyone wants happiness. Everyone wants this sense of fulfillment, and I believe everyone at one time or another has had a taste of being happy. John Maysfield has said "The days that make us happy make us wise." But I believe that almost everyone might have a different definition of what it is that is called *happiness,* and I think that most of us would agree that it is more an attitude than an achievement. It's more a state of mind than a goal to gain. Abraham Lincoln said "People are usually as happy as they make up their minds to be."

With respect to this chapter's theme let me share some other impressions about the meaning of happiness. First, think of how you would feel if you lost everything you have right now, and then, got it all back again. Sometimes I think we would be happier with what we have if we weren't so unhappy about what we don't have. To be happy now, add not to your possessions, but subtract from your desires. The truth of the matter is that happiness comes not so much in having a lot to live on, but in having a lot to live for!

Blessed are the poor in spirit – Heavenly happiness, being blessed, in this beatitude belongs to the spiritually poor. John Wesley believed that the Beatitudes comprise the several stages of the Christian course in life. They reveal the successive steps Christians must take in their journeys to the kingdom, and poverty of spirit is not only the first step, but the root from which all others grow. Real Christianity begins in becoming poor in spirit. This is the foundation of faith, the heart's doorway that opens for the winds of spiritual rebirth to enter in.

The poor in spirit are those who, whatever their circumstances, have an inward disposition that bears the marks of the much-needed first step to all real substantial happiness. The spiritually poor are those who realize they have no spiritual wealth; there is nothing spiritually good within them. The spiritually poor are those who are convinced of the sinfulness of their human condition: They are guilty and ashamed. They see more and more of the faults and flaws that spring from their state of *Fallenness.* Wesley lists some of them: the pride of haughtiness of spirit, the constant bias to think of themselves more highly than they ought to think, vanity, the thirst after the esteem or honor that comes from the praise of others; hate and envy; jealousy and revenge; anger, malice, and bitterness; the love of the world; self-will; and foolish and hurtful desires. The poor in spirit are conscious of how deeply they have offended by their tongue if not by profane, immodest, untrue or unkind words, than by conversations which are not "good for edifying as fits the occasion, that it may impart grace to those who hear" (Ephesians 4:29 ASV). This list could go on and on. The poor in spirit are so encompassed with sin, sorrow, and fear that they are at that desperate point of crying out like a drowning man weary of his struggle, "Lord save me!" Right there is where blessedness begins.

The poor in spirit are aware that all they can do is yield to God in their helplessness. They see more and more of the inward affliction that comes in knowing the true punishment they deserve for their sins. This is spiritual poverty.

But it is so much more. To be poor in spirit can also include the material poverty that knows it's real need. Blessedness is not for those who boast of their poverty, for to do so would make one proud to be humble. It is for those who are free from a love of money; free from coveting their neighbor's house, or wife, or manservant, or maidservant (Exodus 20:17). Such a spiritual poverty refuses the cultural pressure to "keep up with the Joneses." But, Wesley notes, that to be so free from such a love of money and things, to be free of this "root of all evil" (1 Tinothy 6:10), even perhaps by taking a vow of voluntary poverty, does not mean that someone is actually free from *all* evil. There are a thousand roots of evil. John Wesley says that if poverty of spirit were only freedom from coveting, from the love of money, and the desire for riches, it would coincide with or or be a branch of purity of heart – the sixth Beatitude.

But we should still acknowledge the virtue of simplicity as an element of spiritual poverty. I love the old Shaker hymn, *Simple Gifts*:

'Tis the gift to be simple, 'tis the gift to be free,
'tis the gift to come down where you ought to be,
and when we find ourselves in the place just right
it will be in the valley of love and delight.
When true simplicity is gained
to bow and to bend we shant be ashamed.
To turn. turn twill be our delight,
till by turning, turning we come round right.

Being poor is not a blessing. Being simple can be. Being happy with the essentials is a blessing; being satisfied with enough to get by physically, socially, intellectually, and emotionally is a blessing!

There is another dimension of spiritual poverty that is more relevant to us today: Poverty of spirit admits its need, but our culture cultivates the sin of being so proud of spirit that the ignorant phrase "I'm doing fine" becomes a wall. People are starving for attention, for love, for fulfillment and understanding, but they're too proud to admit their need or their sense of lack; their lack of feeling loved, or having the understanding they need so desperately. We lean so far towards self-reliance that it becomes absurd. People would be more friendly and helpful if we weren't always "fine." People who are too proud to admit they're hurting shouldn't be surprised if nobody seems to care, because all they see is the wall of "fine."

But poverty of spirit admits its need. We are helpless sometimes. Which are you: "I've got a problem, can you help me?" "I don't understand, can you enlighten me?" "I don't agree with you, can you compromise?" "I'm lost, can you direct me?" "I'm tired, can you give me strength?" "I'm ready to give up, can you rescue me?" "I'm about to explode, can you calm me down?" "I'm wrong, I'm human, I made a mistake, I prayed, I repent, God forgives me, I forgive myself, I'm sorry, can you forgive me?"

Happiness comes in recognizing your deepest need and then discovering where that need can be supplied. It's like the man in the desert dying of thirst who suddenly sights an oasis, he discovers happiness. And we're all in a spiritual desert. We refuse to admit it, but we're helpless apart from God. Remember you are dust and to dust you shall return.

<u>Theirs is the kingdom of heaven</u> – The ultimate blessing is the kingdom of heaven. And you know what…? it's in our midst! (Luke 17:2). Galatians 5:22 tells us that "the fruit of the spirit is love, joy, peace, patience, kindness, goodness, faithfulness, gentleness, and self-control. Against such there is no law." And what is love but the life of God in the soul, having the mind which was in Christ Jesus. It's the image of God stamped upon the heart. It's the love of God who sent his Son "not to condemn the world but that the world might be saved through him" (John 3:17). And what is joy but the knowing that Jesus died in our place, accepting this, living it out as a child totally dependent upon God for anything good within. It is a state of blessedness. And what is peace but the calm serenity of soul that knows Jesus is our brother. And patience, kindness, goodness, faithfulness, gentleness, and self-control simply follow suit. They are the true needs. These are the things we should desire; these are the objects called precious by the poor in spirit.

Poverty of spirit begins where a sense of guilt and the wrath of God ends; and it's a continual sense of the total dependence on God for every good thought or word or work. Poverty of spirit begins with an admission of need, of helplessness, of desolation. It begins with a recognition that what we are is really nothing to be proud of and then raises within us the desire for grace, the free gift of God. Poverty of spirit comes when we empty ourselves of our pride and sense of self-sufficiency, and let God fill our cup. And blessedness begins when we see that God has poured Himself out for us so graciously that we can say, "My cup runneth over!" (Psalm 23:5 KJV).

THE JOURNEY HOME

Although every journey begins with the first steps in the right direction, here, let's begin by stepping back. We need to take a good look at what is wrong with us. We know something is wrong, because… we are – Here –.

And we don't want to be – Here –. Look at where we are. Was this where we wanted to be?

We are drowning, tired of trying to stay afloat. Maybe we even feel like we're sinking. Maybe a better picture might be that we are up to our neck in quicksand. We cry out for rescue. We need God to throw us a line. And that's exactly when we realize that God has always been there, ready, willing to give us what we need.

The first step is stopping. We need to stop going in the wrong direction. We need to take hold of what will draw us in the right direction. And once that lifeline is in our hands, we begin to feel relief. We begin to trust the saving grace that comes to us in our wretchedness. And right then we begin to envision "home". We can begin to see where we really want to go. We may not know how we'll get there, yet; but, as Christ has said, "theirs is the kingdom of God." When you've got nothing, sometimes, you realize that the Kingdom is there, and that it's really all you want.

The journey home has begun. Now we need to go forward! In the right direction.

SCRIPTURES

To inspire a further consideration of an understanding of poverty of spirit, and, of the kingdom of heaven, here are several relevant passages of Scripture:

Job 42:3-6 – Who is this that hides counsel without knowledge? Therefore I have uttered what I did not understand, things too wonderful for me, which I did not know. Hear, and I will speak; I will question you, and you declare to me. I had heard of you by the hearing of the ear, but now my eyes see you; therefore I despise myself and repent in dust and ashes.

Psalm 40:17 – As for me, I am poor and needy, but the Lord takes thought for me. You are my help and my deliverer; do not delay, O my God

Psalm 34:18 – The Lord is near to those who are brokenhearted, and saves the crushed in spirit.

Psalm 138:6 – For though the Lord is high, he regards the lowly; but the haughty he perceives from far away.

Proverbs 16:18 – Pride goes before destruction, and a haughty spirit before fall.

Proverbs 22:4 – The reward for humility and fear of the Lord is riches and honor and life.

Isaiah 6:5 – And I said, "Woe is me! I am lost, for I am a man of unclean lips, and I live among a people of unclean lips; yet my eyes have seen the King, the Lord of hosts !"

Isaiah 61:1-3 – The spirit of the Lord God is upon me, because the Lord has anointed me; he has sent me to bring good news to the oppressed, to bind up the brokenhearted, to proclaim liberty to the captives, and release to the prisoners; to proclaim the year of the Lord's favor, and the day of vengeance of our God; to comfort all who mourn; to provide for those who mourn in Zion – to give them a garland instead of ashes, the oil of gladness instead of mourning, the mantle of praise instead of a faint spirit. They will be called oaks of righteousness, the planting of the Lord, to display his glory.

Micah 6:8 – He has told you, O mortal, what is good: and what does the Lord require of you but to do justice, and to love kindness, and to walk humbly with your God?

Matthew 11:29 – "Take my yoke upon you, and learn from me; for I am gentle and humble in heart, and you will find rest for your souls."

Matthew 18:3 – "Truly I tell you, unless you change and become like children, you will never enter the kingdom of heaven."

Matthew 18:4 – "Whoever becomes humble like this child is the greatest in the kingdom of heaven."

Matthew 20:26-28 – "It will not be so among you, but whoever wishes to be great among you must be your servant, and whoever wishes to be first among you must be your slave; just as the Son of Man came not to be served but to serve, and to give his life as a ransom for many.

Luke 15:17-19 – But when he came to himself he said. "How many of my father's hired hands have bread enough and to spare, but here I am dying of hunger! I will get up and go to my father, and I will say to him, 'Father, I have sinned against heaven and before you; I am no longer worthy to be called your son; treat me like one of your hired hands.'"

Luke 18:13-14 – "But the tax collector, standing far off, would not even look up to heaven, but was beating his breast and saying, 'God be merciful to me a sinner!' I tell you this man went down to his home justified rather than the other; for all who exalt themselves will be humbled, but all who humble themselves will be exalted."

Romans 7:24-25 – Wretched man that I am! Who will rescue me from this body of death? Thanks be to God through Jesus Christ Our Lord! So then, with my mind I am a slave to the law of God, but with my flesh I am a slave to the law of sin.

Romans 12:3 – For by the grace given to me I say to everyone among you not to think of yourself more highly than you ought to think, but to think with sober judgment, each according to the measure of faith that God has assigned

Philippians 2:3 – Do nothing from selfish ambition or conceit, but in humility regard others as better than yourselves.

Colossians 3:12-15 – As God's chosen ones, holy and beloved, clothe yourself with compassion, kindness, humility, meekness, and patience. Bear with one another and, if anyone has a complaint against another, forgive each other; just as the Lord has forgiven you so you also must forgive. Above all, clothe yourselves with love which binds everything together in perfect harmony; and let the peace of Christ rule in your hearts, to which indeed you were called in the one body. And be thankful.

James 4:6 – But he gives all the more grace; therefore it says, "God opposes the proud, but gives grace to the humble."

James 4:7-10 – Submit yourselves therefore to God. Resist the devil, and he will flee from you. Draw near to God and He will draw near to you. Cleanse your hands, you sinners, and purify your hearts, you double minded. Lament and mourn and weep. Let your laughter be turned into morning and your joy into dejection. Humble yourselves before the Lord and He will exalt you..

1 Peter 5:5b-6 – And all of you must clothe yourselves with humility in your dealings with one another, for "God opposes the proud but gives grace to the humble." Humble yourselves therefore under the mighty hand of God, so that he may exalt you in due time.

WHAT TO DO

Stop going in the wrong direction. That's the first thing.

Look carefully at what you've become. A little self-examination is never a bad idea. It might hurt, but it's the right thing to do.

Realize that <u>you</u> are not your only purpose.

Think about what you would have, even if you lost everything.

Consider the things about you that you'd like to keep. What character traits in you are worthy?

Consider Job. He lost everything!

Think about what gives you hope.

Think about God's kingdom. It is promised to the poor in spirit!

Think about what it might mean to "clothe yourself with humility".

"In humility regard others as better than yourselves." How will you do that?

A PRAYER

O God, I know I need You. Only You can save me from myself. Give me a vision of Your Kingdom, Lord. Help me to hear the words of Christ about Your love, and how He freely took my place on the cross, being punished for my sins, and crucified for my rebellions against Your way. Let me see my poverty and Your wealth. Help me understand the way You want to give so much to me that my cup will overflow. And help me to be grateful. This I pray in Jesus's name. Amen,

A POEM

I May Not Be Much
I may not be much, but somehow I'm here.
It's not where I want to be, and I'm just so full of fear.
I feel so dirty. I just want to get clean.
I feel so sad. I hate what I've seen.
The path I have followed,
The poison I've swallowed
Has made my heart sick, my mind is confused
There must be a pathway I just haven't used.
I hope I can find it. I sure need it now.
And if there's a way, I will get there somehow.
A fog has been lifted. Now I can see.
I need some direction to what I can be.
I need to envision a purpose that's right.
I need to begin to follow the Light.

CHAPTER TWO

THOSE WHO MOURN

Blessed are those who mourn,
for they will be comforted.
Matthew 5:4

The Beatitudes – Rules for living are around almost every corner. We have the Ten Commandments. Every society has laws. Different groups have principles by which they aspire to live. There are moral codes and disciplines, philosophies and theories, beliefs and reasonings, and even many unspoken rules of etiquette, all determined to help us to be the best we should be. The Beatitudes are a wonderful list that can help to bring order to human behavior. We need them. And in the midst of all the possibilities, the Beatitudes seem to turn things upside down.

Blessing – In the first chapter about The Beatitudes, we began considering the first and the foundation of them all: "Blessed are the poor in spirit, for theirs is the kingdom of heaven." It is theirs because, in feeling their desperate need for the kingdom, they get it. That's the way God seems to work. God meets our real needs, and the poor in spirit have given up any trust they ever had in their own abilities to save themselves. In fact, the poor in spirit have given up relying on *things* completely, and they have have given up relying on themselves. All that is left for them in their spiritual poverty is their need to rely on God, and, until we can yield to God, until we, in our poverty of spirit, become beggars of the spirit, the kingdom cannot be ours. So it becomes natural to grieve. We mourn the fact that, without God, and without faith, there is no hope.

<u>The Mournful</u> – The second Beatutude says: "*Blessed are those who mourn, for they shall be comforted.*" This becomes the first offspring of our spiritual poverty, and our turning and facing the direction of home. Having seen our own desperation, we have turned to God, and then we turn toward home. Looking again at the world around us, we see our misery and the state of all human misery. Everyone's desperation intensifies itself into grief.

But there is a blessedness in such mournfulness. Ironically implied is that there is a joy in sorrow. Jesus never claimed that grief was a blessing, but in Psalm 51:17 we are reminded that "*the sacrifice acceptable to God is a broken spirit; a broken and contrite heart, O God, You will not despise.*" Grief may not be a blessing, but there are blessings in grief.

To a world that says, "Eat, drink, and be merry, for tomorrow we die," (Luke 12:19), Christ says "Grieve, for today, and tomorrow many will still suffer." We should never be content with an unexamined life, or, an unexamined world. The real beginning of spiritual Christianity is an utter dissatisfaction with life as it is, evoking a sorrow that pierces the heart with the intensity of mourning, plunging us into a feeling that hurts so much that we don't want to suffer it. We don't want anyone to have to feel this way. Comfort must come or we will die. And that's the promise of this Beatitude: <u>Comfort</u>!

But this mournfulness is due to the shocking realization of our own sin and of the sinfulness of the world. Therefore the answer is at hand: Repent! Penitence. Unless penitence begins, the grief becomes an overwhelming burden, we are not only broken, we are crushed. And only God can put the pieces of our lives back together. With God the darkness of our world can reveal the starlight of the heavens. Paul said in 2 Corinthians 7:10 that "*Godly grief produces a repentance that leads to salvation and brings no regret, but worldly grief produces death.*" The sorrow of penitence is the doorway to the joy of forgiveness and reconciliation.

I mentioned the sense of dissatisfaction with life as it is. Today, too many people are satisfied, and, if they're not, they're either dissatisfied and indifferent, disaffected, or detached; or, they just don't know what can be done; or, they have just given up and figured that this is just the way things are. And maybe, they're detached just enough not to be looking for a better way. Still our sadness should make us better, not bitter.

One of the first responses to grief is denial. We sometimes think the problem is not true, or, real. So we deny that it even exists. We just don't *want* to believe the problem even exists. But then begins a ritual of blaming. We should learn, however, that when something has gone wrong, we shouldn't be looking for someone or something to blame, but for the solution to the problem. Turn your problems into projects! Sometimes, though, we'll even want to blame God! Job didn't blame God. His reaction was, *"The Lord gives and the Lord has taken away. Blessed be the name of the Lord!"* (Job 1:21). Job stood fast in his integrity, and in the integrity of God.

In our grief there can also be anger … a feeling of wanting to fight back. Rather than merely accepting defeat, we want to rebell against the pain. Out of such a feeling can come a new resolve, a renewed hope. Sorrow motivates us to rethink our attitudes. Through our morning we can begin to discover what really matters, as well as what doesn't matter. A little girl lost her doll and was sad. Her father bought her a new doll to try to cheer her up. It didn't work. The father came to talk to the girl, he said he wanted to make her feel better. The little girl said, "Just hug me." Through sorrow, we can discover the meaning of friendship, the meaning of love. *Things* don't really seem to matter. And when your values begin to change, your whole life can start to change too!

"For everything there is a season… a time to weep, and a time to laugh" (Ecclesiastes 3:1, 4). Sorrow has its place. One of the unique blessings that can come through our grief is that we can discover whether our faith is a real foundation, or, a superficial ornament. And still, sometimes, when you hit bottom, you can find God. It's as if God is all that is left.

Contrast the blessedness of those who mourn with the depression of those who never express their sorrow or grief, who hold in all their brokenness. If we accept the present toil and the present tears, we will be able to know the ultimate and permanent joy. We must be sensitive, though, because sometimes sadness builds unintended barriers. My sadness might make you hold back. We've been conditioned to assume that the only normal state of being is cheerfulness. We don't always know what to do when another adult cries, and even though we may sympathize, we hold it in and try to lie and say, "It's all right." "Everything's fine". but… "Just hug me."

It's not all right. we are not fine. if we choose to live as if nothing really mattered beyond this moment, then all we will get is what this moment has to offer. But if we choose to live with the conviction that there is something far more important beyond us now, the whole world will seem more meaningful. We will grieve when this is denied.

Blessed are those who mourn. Mourners do not just weep with those who weep (Romans 12:15), they have a deep concern. Mourners will weep even for those who do not weep for themselves, but should. They are not only mournful over their own personal guilt, but over their neighbors sins, and over the wickedness of the world. The mournful that are blessed are grieving with God! They are troubled over those who still walk in darkness. They are hurt by all the dishonor being done continually to the majesty of the Kingdom of Heaven! ...over the world's indifference to it... and over the way Christ's grace is so taken for granted.

Blessedness belongs to those who grieve over the sin, the sadness, and the suffering of this world. It belongs to those who are touched by others in the midst of *their* mourning, In the midst of *their* tears. Their sense of justice is quickened. They are challenged by the suffering, the oppression, and the injustice inflicted upon the meek of the world. There's a genuine concern for the bankrupt condition of humanity. The appeal for help, whether spoken or never given voice is not left unheard by them. People need you! A person's attitude toward Christ is revealed in their attitude toward "the least of these." The concern in our hearts compels us to action. It urges us to reach out. It inspires us to serve. This is an effect of the kind of mourning that brings a blessing. Service is its result. It cares enough to want to make a difference. It inspires compassion, like the Good Samaritan.

Cool detachment becomes a curse. but one who mourns is grieved enough to give up their own comfort to try to comfort another. Such a person was Mother Theresa. Such a person is promised final comfort. Such a person is blessed.

They shall be comforted – People who weep with those who weep will bring to others a comfort, not a comparison to their own grieving. They will bring compassion, not euphemisms. They will bring companionship, not camaraderie. They will bring calm, not tension. Theirs is a presence, not a pity. And we must all be willing to accept the blessings of comfort that God is offering to others through our caring arms, and to us through the caring arms of others.

Like parents never leaving a young child alone at the hospital, God is always by our side to comfort us. Comfort gives us courage. God enables us to face the future. We must let our dreams be shaped by hope, not by hurt. We shouldn't dwell on what devastates us, on what we've lost, or, on what we now lack. We should think, rather, about what is left: Life! And life is a garden, judge it by the flowers, not by the leaves that fall!

Godly comfort can be seen in the open arms of the Prodigal father, glad to see his penitent son return. It is consoling, like a divine hug, and underneath are the everlasting arms! Godly comfort is the difference between being devastated and isolated, to being cared for in community. "Who shall separate us from the love of Christ?" (Romans 8:35-39) Nothing shall separate us from the love of God in Christ Jesus our Lord.

THE JOURNEY HOME

The Prodigal has set his eyes not only on "home," but on the merciful eyes of his father. His father will feel pity when he sees him. He will feel disappointment, at least to some degree, maybe even a lot; but he will see his son's return as his hope to start over, to make amends, to turn over a new leaf in his life. The father has already been grieving over his son. To him, it's as if his son was dead. But he is coming back to life.

The Prodigal needs pity. He believes in his father's kindness enough to know he will accept him, at least, as a servant, a hired hand. The father knows his son has been foolish. He knows the instant he sees him that he was lost in his wasteful living. Perhaps he even sees his son as having betrayed the ideals that nurtured him from his childhood. We can do everything possible to instill righteousness in our children, but they can still make poor decisions.

But the best decision is to come home!

We need to be this Prodigal father. We need to have pity and mercy for those who are lost, who have hit bottom and feel like there is no where else to go. The Church is the Prodigal father. We welcome people home. We embrace them even though they seemed lost and rejectable. They are grieving over their sinful condition, and so do we. God wants to comfort them, and we are the comforters. Through us, God brings comfort and welcome to the Prodigal. How beautiful to see ourselves in this way. We are "home"!

SCRIPTURES

To inspire a further consideration of an understanding of grief and mourning here are several relevant passages of Scripture:

Psalm 23:4 – Even though I walk through the valley of the shadow of death, I fear no evil; for you are with me; your rod and your staff they comfort me .

Psalm 34:18 – The Lord is near to the brokenhearted, and saves the crushed in spirit

Psalm 73:26 – My Flesh and my heart may fail, but God is the strength of my heart and my portion forever

Psalm 116:8 – For you have delivered my soul from death, my eyes from tears, my feet from stumbling.

Psalm 147:3 – He heals the brokenhearted, and binds up their wounds.

Proverbs 3:5-6 –Trust in the Lord with all your heart, and do not rely in your own insight. In all your ways acknowledge Him, and He will make straight your paths.

Isaiah 25:8 – He will swallow up death forever. Then the Lord God will wipe away the tears from all faces, and the disgrace of his people he will take away from all the earth, for the Lord has spoken.

Isaiah 40:10 – Behold the Lord comes with might, his arm rules for him; his reward is with him, and his recompense before him.

John 11:25-26 – Jesus said to her, "I am the resurrection and the life. Those who believe in me, even though they die, will live, and everyone who lives and believes In me will never die. Do you believe this?"

John 14:7 – "If you know me, you will know my father also. From now on you do know him and have seen him."

Romans 8:18 – I consider that the sufferings of this present time are not worth comparing with the glory about to be revealed to us.

Romans 8:38-39 – I am convinced that neither death, nor life, nor angels, nor rulers, nor things present, nor things to come, nor powers, nor height, nor depth, or anything else in all creation, will be able to separate us from the love of God in Christ Jesus our lord

2 Corinthians 1:3-4 – Blessed be the God and father of our Lord Jesus Christ, the father of mercies and the God of all consolation, who consoles us in our affliction, so that we may be able to console those who are in any affliction with the consolation with which we ourselves are consoled by God.

2 Corinthians 5:8 – Yes, we do have confidence, and we would rather be away from the body and at home with the Lord.

Revelation 21:4 – He will wipe away every tear from their eyes, Death will be no more; mourning and crying and pain will be no more, for the first things have passed away

WHAT TO DO

Do not fear. Have confidence.

Think: What moral code do you live by?

Consider the things on which you have relied; like good works, self-determination, positive thinking, etc.

See your misery, and the miserable state of all human misery.

Why is *the sacrifice acceptable to God a broken spirit*? What does that mean to you?

Consider: "The real beginning of spiritual Christianity is an utter dissatisfaction with life as it is, evoking a sorrow that pierces the heart with the intensity of mourning, plunging us into a feeling that hurts so much that we don't want to suffer it. We don't want anyone to have feel this way." Is this true? Do you agree? How do you feel when you look upon the problems and difficulties of our world?

Do you feel a "sense of dissatisfaction with life as it is" ?

Don't place blame. Even if you can think of someone or something to blame, realize that blaming never helps!

Choose to live with the conviction that there is something far more important beyond us now.

Consider how you are challenged by the suffering, the oppression, and the injustice inflicted upon the people of this world. What do you want to do about it?

Be like the Prodigal father.

A PRAYER

O mighty God, by whose strength the weak are made able, by whose guidance the lost find a way, and by whose mercy the sinful know forgiveness: You have made us conquerors through Jesus Christ, and yet we have too often retreated in a spirit of defeat. We have let the things of this world separate us from the love we can know in Christ Jesus our Lord. We confess that we have forgotten Your merciful ways, we have neglected Your guidance, and we have thought we could carry on in our own strength without You.

Forgive us, we pray, renew in us an urgent longing for Your ways. Inspire in us a great zeal for Your glory. And ignite in us the great fire of Your Spirit, till we are one in love, striving to know Your Kingdom in our midst.

This we pray in Jesus's holy Name. Amen.

A POEM

It's So Sad to Know The Glorious Light

It's so sad to know the glorious light
  While darkness somehow seems to reign
And dawn's arrived after a night
   where loss and sorrow brought you pain
    And no one seems to watch the sky

A great new morning has begun
  It keeps beginning every day
But all too few have seen the sun
   Arising with it's perfect ray
    While no one lets the darkness die.

It grieves the heart whose vision calls
  To tell the world the needed word
About the sunshine past the squalls
   That blot out voices left unheard.
    And no one lets the mouners cry.

A SONG

DON'T WEEP
(With a nod to "The Green Fields of France")

O the past is only prologue, and our memories are sweet;
and the journeys we are taking they may still seem incomplete
But the sacrifices offered in the best parts of our years
Are worth our every wound and our every hour of tears.

We may sometimes feel lonely, we may sometimes want a change
We may sometimes wish the paths we took could just be rearranged
There may be some regrets and there may be some remorse
We may wish we had chased some dreams and tried another course

But here we are, and here's our fate, and here's to marching on;
And here's to all the memories of old days done and gone

    Refrain:

Don't weep for the righteous. Don't weep for the holy.
        Don't weep for the blest who have finished their race.
But weep for the broken ones lost in their folly,
        And weep for the rebels rejecting God's grace.

The pain that we are feeling when our days are almost done
Is more for what we didn't do than for how the race was run
We sometimes have been foolish but we got a second chance
And we smiled and we laughed when we danced another dance

    Refrain...

Now let's sing all the songs that can make us feel free
For they echo with the questions and the answers we need
The past that we remember is a burden to some
But the future is unwritten and the best is yet to come

    Refrain...

CHAPTER THREE

THE MEEK

Blessed are the meek, for they will inherit the earth.
Matthew 5:5

<u>The Beatitudes</u> – Authentic discipleship is what is described in the Beatitudes. What makes something authentic? Jesus describess an authentic disciple as "the salt of the earth" and, "the light of the world" (Matthew 5:13, 14). A disciple's authenticity is sometimes determined by the taste and by the vision they help to bring to the world. Those received into eternity in the Parable of the Great Judgment in Matthew 25:31-46 are those who serve "the least" in the world. (v. 39). Jesus is teaching Kingdom principles, not worldly wisdom. We should never intellectualize the faith. We need to let faith have a place. Authenticity is a legitimizing of God's ultimate purposes. It makes God real. And it makes God's kingdom real.

A big issue of our day is the idea of fact-checking. Knowing the actual facts brings a legitimacy to what we say. If what we say does not agree with the facts, then we are lacking in legitimacy. Integrity comes into question. We need to be true to the Truth.

<u>Blessing</u> – An ultimate sort of happiness is promised in the Beatitudes. Our best life is what is intended. All too often we are short-sighted when it comes to happiness/blessedness. We tend to think only of "my" happiness, or "our" happiness, not realizing that the greatest source of happiness is to bring happiness into the lives of others. But the joys of belief and the heart-warming goodness of faith are so enriching that we should hunger

for them, we should thirst for them. But first, let's examine what it means to be meek.

<u>Blessed Are The Meek</u> – The Blessed mournful become the blessed meek. And if meekness evokes the image of a doormat, someone people can walk all over (though this image is not meekness), then the blessing of God becomes the obvious response to a desperate need. But the meek should never be considered to be just a spiritless weaklings, unable to help themselves. No, they are surrendered. The meek may include the infirm and disabled or the physically weak and incapacitated; for such the blessing of God is the necessary response to a desperate need. God blesses them and cares for them and gives them the earth as an inheritance. Such people do have a meekness and they are blessed in their physical and spiritual poverty. Still meekness should never be seen as a watered down spinelessness, but rather a solid sort of steadfastness. The meek are not timid, they are able. Able to accept God's grace for their lives; and able to do what God calls on them to do. If they become inheritors, they must also be responsible with what comes to them.

One impression of meekness comes from a nice little song:

> Gentle Jesus, meek and mild…
> Look upon a little child,
> Pity my simplicity,
> Suffer me to come to Thee.

The image is so sweet. We are inspired to be simple, like a child that wants to come to Christ. Jesus is portrayed as a lamb, welcoming mercifrully all who would come to Him. None of this is wrong, but the song tends to leave us equating meekness with mildness, and that is a bit short-sighted. Meekness can easily be connected with mildness, but the thread is weak. It almost seems as if the meek would not be strong, but only sweet, kind, and comforting. All good images, and yet incomplete. Stay with me.

Psalm 37:10-11 says "Yet a little while and the wicked will be no more; though you look well at their place, they will not be there; but the meek shall possess the land and delight themselves in abundant prosperity." Psalm 147:8 says: "The Lord lifts up those who are bowed down."

The meek are not submissive to man, but surrendered to God. The meek are not defiant, but humble and obedient. They are respectful and righteous. They may not be bold or extroverted or outwardly active all the time; but kindly mannered, easy going, and modest in their activities. Needing guidance the meek are accepting of God's ways. The meek, in Christ's mind, as he proclaims the promises of the Beatitudes, are the followers, those who identify with a crowd and have no need to stand out. Like a young bronc, the meek have been broken, and so are able to receive training. The meek are the disciples learning to be faithful. The meek know their strengths, especially the strength of their Master; but they also know their weaknesses – without their Master they are lost.

Among the meek there is a patience, a contendedness, a calm. There's a sense of faithful resignation; not a giving up, but a calm acquiescence to the will of God concerning them. The meek reveal a divine sort of temperament in that their zeal is tempered by knowledge; their eagerness is tempered by understanding, and their fear is tempered by trust. The meek are not after power, but are after justice. They do not claim rights for themselves, but stick to their duty. They do not seek revenge, but let bygones be bygones. The meek are able to overcome evil with good (Romans 12:21).

Job was meek when he was able to say, "The Lord gave, and the Lord has taken away; blessed be the name of the Lord" (Job 1:21). Mary was meek when she was able to say, "Here I am the servant of the Lord; let it be with me according to your word" (Luke 1:38). And Jesus Himself said, "I am meek and lowly in heart" (Matthew 11:29 KJV). He also said, "Whoever wishes to be great among you, must be your servant" (Matthew 20:26). And when he prayed for his cup of suffering to pass he said, "Yet, not my will but yours be done" (Luke 22:42). Carol Kingery was meek.

The meek walk the middle ground between excess and poverty, but do not feel poor nor are they proud. They are simply simple! The meek walk a middle ground between recklessness and cowardice, they are stable. And they are loyal. The meek walk a middle ground between excessive anger and angerlessness, they are kind, gentle, and hopeful. The meek walk a middle ground between bitterness and excessive light-heartedness. They understand. The meek walk a middle ground between being hasty and being slow tempered. They are tranquil and temperate. The meek walk a middle ground between pride and self abasement; theirs is a modesty, a joy. The meek walk a middle ground between doubt and overconfidence; they are secure and trusting. The meek have a quiet sort of courage. The meek are not overly ambitious, except in how they want to please God. They won't show an abundance of zeal, but neither are they lazy; they are constant, steadfast. They are neither bullies, nor do they get pushed around; they are stalwart. The meek are neither extremely opinionated, nor timid, but moderate. The meek are neither fearful nor courageous; but they are committed

The meek are the opposite of the aggressive and defiant. The will of the meek becomes the will of God, nothing more. The meek are pleasing to God, because their greatest wish is to please Him. The meek live out the words of the Lord's Prayer" "thy will be done on earth as it is in heaven." That's why their inheritance is the earth.

They Shall Inherit The Earth – The meek are promised an inheritance. Jesus says they will receive the earth, the land. But what is meant by the word is not a territory, but a place to belong. There is a legacy of the meek. Because they belong, the land usurped by aggressors is rightfully theirs. The aggressors will eventually disappear either through God's uncompromising judgment or through their own undoing, because aggressors are divided against themselves, and at odds with each other. They will destroy themselves. The meek will always be there. The aggressors will fade away. This is the will of God on earth as it is stated in The Magnificat where Mary says, "He has scattered the proud in the imagination of their hearts, he has put down the mighty from their thrones, and exalted those of low degree" (Luke 1:51-52).

The meek find a place, a place of peace. Their legacy is not a position of power, not returning persecution for persecution, but returning peace in any circumstance. The meek have let the love of Christ control them for they are convinced that Christ has died for all, and they know that he died that those who live might no longer live for themselves but for him (2 Corinthians 5:14-15). As we approach meekness, we are beginning to please God.

The Poor in Spirit, The Mournful, and The Meek

A final word about these first three Beatitudes. These are the three great stages of turning toward God. At first we are stopped in our tracks and find no good in ourselves. We are spiritually bankrupt. Then, realizing this we hurt enough to grieve, and the only thing we can do is turn to God for help. And finally, we begin to meekly set our minds on the will of God.

You may say that you turned toward God long, long ago. Now the spirit has made you bold, not meek; your faith has brought you joy, not mourning. Your heart is rich in Christ, not poor in spirit. Come then, let us test and examine our ways to see if there is any evil within us. Without God we are nothing. Remember you are dust and to dust you shall return! Repent and believe the gospel! Repent, and hunger and thirst for righteousness, for then you will be pleased again; you'll be blessed again; you will be satisfied. You will be faithful.

THE JOURNEY HOME

At the time of Christ, the only people who had maps were leaders of armies and ruling officials. Common people didn't have maps. They may have known about some of the main roads, but would have had little clues about where particular towns might be. The popular method of finding your way was to get directions from people along the way. There might have been occasional markers that pointed toward some fairly large cities. But unless you knew something more about exactly where you were going, as in the proximity of your home from the larger towns, and, the orientation of your roads, travel was rarely easy. Many joined groups of travelers on foot who were going in the same direction.

The Prodigal has set his eyes on "home." We who hear the story have no idea where he is in his "lost" condition or where "home" is, but we can sense his need for guidance. Maybe the journey will be direct, maybe it will be somewhat difficult to negotiate every necessary turn. But, we believe he will know which way to go. Have you ever given directions? Did you help those who asked?

My first night in Paris back in 1977, two other Americans from our group, the other guys, and I took a walk. I had suggested we keep our adventure simple. Go straight one way for a mile or so, turn around and come straight back. We knew where our hotel was from the main boulevard, and we could return there easily. It was two left turns from a certain corner, and all we had to do was remember the street names.

About a mile north, some guys in a car, pulled up nearby. One guy got out, approached a few steps, and asked, in French, where the West Station (Gare L'Ouest) was. I chuckled, at first because they had no clue that we might be foreigners, and, second, because I remembered seeing a sign that pointed the way to Gare L'Ouest! I could give directions to someone in Paris! I told him, in French, that there was a sign back *that* way, as I pointed south. The guy thanked me, got back in the car, and they drove off in that direction.

The Prodigal needed directions. We need to do more than just tell someone who is lost that they are "lost". We need to give them directions.

SCRIPTURES

To inspire a further consideration of an understanding of meekness, and, of the kingdom of heaven, here are several relevant passages of Scripture:

Isaiah 53:7 – He was oppressed, and he was afflicted, yet he did not open his mouth; like a lamb that is led to the slaughter, and like sheep that before it's shearers is silent so, he did not open his mouth.

Jeremiah 26:14 – But as for me, here I am in your hands. Do with me as seems good and right to you.

Matthew 11:29 – Take my yoke up on you, and learn from me; for I am gentle and humble in heart, and you will find rest for your souls.

Matthew 21:5 – "Tell the daughter of Zion, Look. your king is coming to you humble, and mounted on a donkey and on a colt, the full of a donkey."

Matthew 26:52 – Then Jesus said to him, "Put your sword back into its place; for all who take the sword will perish by the sword."

1 Corinthians 4:11-13a – To the present hour we are hungry and thirsty, we are poorly clothed and beaten and homeless, and we grow weary from

the work of our own hands. When reviled we bless; when persecuted we endure; when slandered, we speak kindly.

2 Corinthians 10:1 – I myself, Paul, appeal to you by the meekness and gentleness of Christ – I who am humble when face-to-face with you, but bold toward you when I am away.

Ephesians 4:1-3 – I therefore, the prisoner in the Lord, beg you to lead a life worthy of the calling to which you have been called, with all humility and gentleness, with patience, bearing with one another in love, making every effort to maintain the unity of the spirit in the bond of peace.

Philippians 2:5-8 – Let the same mind be among you that was in Christ Jesus, who, though he was in the form of God, did not regard equality with God as something to be exploited, but emptied himself, taking the form of a slave, being born in human likeness. And being found in human form, he humbled himself and became obedient to the point of death – even death on a cross.

Colossians 3:12 – As God's chosen ones, holy and beloved, clothe yourselves with compassion, kindness, humility, meekness, and patience.

2 Timothy 2:24-25 – And the Lord's servant must not be quarrelsome but kindly to everyone, an apt teacher, patient, correcting opponents with gentleness. God May perhaps grant that they will repent and come to know the truth.

1 Thessalonians 2:7 – ...though we might have made demands as Apostles of Christ. But we were gentle among you like a nurse tenderly caring for her own children

Titus 3:1-2 – Remind them to be subject to rulers and authorities, to be obedient, to be ready for every good work, to speak evil of no one, to avoid quarreling, to be gentle, and to show every courtesy to everyone.

1 Peter 3:4 – Let your adornment be the inner self with the lasting beauty of a gentle and quiet spirit, which is very precious in God's sight.

1 Peter 3:15 – But in your hearts sanctify Christ as Lord. Always be ready to make your defense to anyone who demands from you and accounting for the hope that is in you.

James 3:17 – The wisdom from above is first pure, then peaceable, gentle, willing to yield, full of mercy and good fruits, without a trace of partiality or hypocrisy.

WHAT TO DO

Be gentle. Being gentle is not being weak.

Measure the authenticity of your discipleship. On a scale of 1 to 10, one being completely inauthentic and ten being totally authentic, where do you see yourself?

Reflect: Never intellectualize the faith. What does that mean?

Consider the issue of legitimacy. What makes faith, thoughts, ideas legitimate?

Reflect: What images does the word "meek" conjure up in your mind?

Revisit this sentence: "The meek are not submissive to man, but surrendered to God." What does it mean to be submissive? What does it mean to be surrendered?

Be obedient.

Try to say with Christ: "Yet, not my will but yours be done" (Luke 22:42).

Put your life in God's hands.

Bear with one another in love.

Make every effort to maintain the unity of the spirit in the bond of peace.

Consider what it means to "have a place to belong."

A PRAYER

Almighty God, You have been gentle with us even when we have been harsh with others; You are kind even when we have been mean; and You have been easy on us even when we have been difficult; give us a place to belong and help us seek Your will in all things. Let us be steadfast and stalwart; let us be determined, but resigned; and let us be a sign of Your strength. Give us modesty and resilience. We put ourselves into Your hands and ask for You to use us as You desire. This we pray in Jesus's name. Amen.

A POEM

THE MEEK

Quiet courage describes the meek –
Loyal in their duty, tenacious as they seek –
Silently heroic, steadfast to their call –
Solid with a leg-up to overcome a wall.
Positive, persistent, but never all that proud –
Maybe not a leader, but the strength of every crowd.

Let us all be meek, then, for we will be defined
As righteous and surrendered and generous and kind.
By simple resignation to the leading of God's will,
We would be a sign of trust, of service, and of skill.

O to be forgiven! Glad to be redeemed –
Calm in our contentedness, blessed in our esteem,

Let us be the meek, then, in the midst of God's defense –
Soldiers who are ready for God's battle to commence!

CHAPTER FOUR

THOSE WHO HUNGER AND THIRST

Blessed are those who hunger and thirst for righteousness,
For they will be filled.
Matthew 5:6

The Beatitudes

What's the one thing you'd like to have more than anything else in the whole world? Is it righteousness? "Blessed are those who hunger and thirst for righteousness, for they shall be satisfied" (NASB)!

Goals are relevant. A person with no goals in life probably would have little hope. Having goals can give us a reason to live. Wanting to accomplish something can give us a goal to look forward, a sense of direction. The Beatitudes in Christ's Sermon on the Mount are more than rules for living, though they are indeed exactly that; they each have a promise attached to them. So far the promises include the Kingdom of Heaven, comfort, inheriting the earth, and, with this chapter, satisfaction, fulfillment. And just as the journey includes the vision of the destination and the feeling of being there already, so too do the promises of the Beatitudes, include the sense of their fulfillment.

Imagine some of the things in your life that make you happy. Make a quick list. Thank God for these things. Count your blessings. Seek those things. The things that make us happy are blessings. You are already blessed in so many ways

<u>Blessing</u> – Blessedness, or, happiness is said to be like sunshine – they who bring sunshine into the lives of others cannot keep it from themselves. Greta Palmer once said that happiness is a byproduct of an effort to make someone else happy. So bringing light into the lives of others would likewise brighten our own lives. Expanding on the idea of happiness being a byproduct, it becomes possible to say that happiness is like warmth, and by bringing warmth into the lives of others you cannot help but become warmer yourself. And remember Charlie Brown says that happiness is a warm puppy! It's also possible to say that happiness is like peace or kindness or love, by bringing such things into the lives of others, you cannot keep them from yourself. And to tie this idea into the issue of fulfillment, perhaps happiness is also like wholeness/fulfillment – the more you work to bring wholeness into the lives of others, the more it is likely to rub off on you; and you would be whole.

<u>They Shall Be Satisfied</u> – Wholeness. The word *satisfied* In this passage means whole, or, complete. It does not mean *satisfactory* as in "just getting by". To be truly satisfied means to fulfill a potential. Satisfaction for a cup would be to be full. In human terms, satisfaction would be the quality that would make you more fully able to be yourself. Of course, for people we can almost never know final satisfaction. Human nature is such that once we have acquired the potential in one aspect of our lives, it almost always seems that some new horizons open up to us. We *can* find brief moments of satisfaction and wholeness, at times, but once we've achieved one goal, another looms up before us. We are able to grow constantly. The moment we stop growing we start dying.

They shall be satisfied, fulfilled. What is that sort of satisfaction? What is real satisfaction, that feeling of being complete? For some it might be a sort of conquest – reaching the highest high, catching the biggest catch… For others it might be just being on the mountainside, or just being on the river. Realize, however, that these earthly satisfactions are always only temporary; and realize too that this Beatitude promises satisfaction not for the righteous but for those who *hunger* and *thirst* for it.

So what makes us feel fulfilled? What is there that gives us a sense of soundness and integrity? Can our lives ever come to know that feeling of being entirely all together, or, will there always seem to be another piece of the puzzle to put into place? It seems, to me, like this is so.

<u>Those Who Hunger and Thirst</u> – The requirement Jesus poses for this blessing of satisfaction is not the attainment of righteousness as I have said, but the hunger and thirst for it. It's not just the good intention that counts, for intentions breed action; or, at least, they should breed action. It's the sense of commitment, the depth of the desire that reveals an intensity that could only be described as hunger or thirst

And our souls are starving! How do we feed them? Our spirits languish with thirst. What can refresh them? We need the bread of faith and the cup of blessing that only Jesus offers. His blessing is to those who long for righteousness as much as a starving man longs for food, and as much as a thirsty man longs for water. Consider John 4:7-15 – "A Samaritan woman came to draw water, and Jesus said to her, 'Give me a drink.' (His disciples had gone into the city to buy food.) The Samaritan woman said to him, 'How is it that you, a Jew, ask a drink of me, a woman of Samaria?' (Jews did not share things in common with Samaritans). Jesus answered her, 'If you knew the gift of God and who it is that is saying to you "give me a drink", you would have asked him, and he would have given you living water.' The woman said to him, 'Sir, you have no bucket and the well is deep. Where do you get that living water? Are you greater than our ancestor Jacob, who gave us the well and with his sons and his flocks drank from it?' Jesus said to her, 'Everyone who drinks this water will be thirsty again, but those who drink of the water that I will give them will never be thirsty. The water that I will give will become in them a spring of water gushing up to eternal life.' The woman said to him, 'Sir give me this water so that I may never be thirsty or have to keep coming here to draw water.'"

Consider also John 6:35 -- "Jesus said to them, 'I am the bread of life; whoever comes to me will never be hungry, and whoever believes in me will never be thirsty."

The image of hungering and thirsting for God in this beatitude is not new. In Psalm 42: 1-2, it says, "As a hart longs for flowing streams so longs my soul for thee, O God; my soul thirsts for God for the living God." In Psalm 63:1 it says, "O God, thou art my God. I seek thee, my soul thirsts for thee; my flesh faints for thee as in a dry and weary land where no water is."

Realize that hunger and thirst are a threat to life; so likewise the spiritually empty will perish eternally! There is a serious threat there. But

Jesus promises their fullness if only they know their true hunger, if only they know their true thirst. If you desire something enough you will do whatever you can to get it. This beatitude makes that promise. You will persevere until you find it; you will persist until you have it; and you will sacrifice everything just to ease your hunger, to quench your thirst.

Realize too that each one of us suffers from some kind of emotional or spiritual hunger and thirst. We constantly want something more. Something is missing in our lives, and that hunger leaves us weak. We're ready to try anything. We're like the person getting up in the middle of the night not knowing what to have, but wanting something, anything. They go to the refrigerator and nibble at this and they try that. Nothing really satisfies Sometimes they eat until they are sick.

And that's the state of our world today. People have tried just about everything to find satisfaction, to be fulfilled, and society is sick. And that sickness makes us even more desperate. We hunger and thirst for all the wrong things, and still we are empty. And in that emptiness people turn to drugs, to crime, to immoral pleasures that only leave them emptier and emptier, until, at times, the only way out of the desolation of their emptiness seems, for too many, to be death.

Back in 1987 suicide among youth in the USA occurred at the incredible rate of an average of about 13 a day, and for every suicide there were about 100 attempts at suicide. 2021 statistices tell us that people 10-24 years old account for 14% of all suicides—surpassing 6,500 deaths each year, which makes suicide the third leading cause of death for this age group. Why? Because they're hungry, they're thirsting for something, something more; and they're just not finding it. And the last place they want to look is in the church.

But I believe with all my heart that the church has the answer, because the answer is Jesus Christ and the kingdom of God. And until we as the church begin to live with the conviction that we truly wanted eternal life as much as a starving man wants food or as much as one dying of thirst wants water, until then there will only remain a vacant emptiness for those who are searching. Another part of the problem is that modern society has become geared to instant gratification. You push a button, there's your need – fast food, instant money, automatic everything; credit cards – buy now, pay later. And it's not only the younger generation but all of us – we don't really learn or practice the true value of things, and many of us have even forgotten the value of faith. What is faith in these modern times? It only seems like something old fashioned. It's not cool. But the kingdom of God, though it may not seem cool now, this very instant, is the coolest. Just like with the mountain top, though, we need to climb, we need to study, to learn, and practice what it means to be faithful. You see faith should never be a matter of interest and attraction, but a hungry craving and driving thirst. The Christian does not say, "I am interested in Christ", but, "For me, to live is Christ" (Philippians 1:21). The Christian does not say, "I would like an arrangement with Christ," but "I surrender my life to Christ." I surrender my life to Christ.

Blessedness – Blessed are those who hunger and thirst for righteousness. This is the most demanding of all the Beatitudes, but also the kindest and most encouraging. Blessedness is not a promise to those who only want to live their own lives and do no harm; it is for those who desire righteousness as a matter of life and death.

In the novel Quo Vadis there's a depiction of a young Roman called Vicinius. He is in love with a Christian girl, but because he is a pagan, she will not return his love. Without her knowledge, he followed her to a little secret gathering of the Christians and, there, he heard Peter preach. As he listened, something happened within him. He came to know that Jesus Christ was the most important reality in life but, "He felt that if he wished to follow his teaching, he would have to place on a burning pile all his thoughts, habits, and character, his whole nature up to that very moment, burn them to ashes, then fill himself with a life altogether different, and, an entirely new soul." Right there and then he made a decision. In every life, there comes such a moment of decision. It may not always be so dramaric. But it can be a very remarkable moment. A turning point.

Vicinius may not have known it but at that very moment, at the very beginning of his turning, he became blessed. He was blessed because the promise of being satisfied is not for those who have finally attained righteousness, but for those who hunger and thirst for it; for those who hunger and thirst for justice. They realize that knowing a personal vindication is not enough. It's not the end of the story, but the beginning. Because the blessed mournfulness from the second Beatitude will return even after we feel we are acceptable before God. Why? Because we will be all the more aware of sin and the lost condition of humankind. And our hunger, our thirst, the cause we want to fight for, will be a total righteousness. The righteousness of all. The righteousness of the world. And we will grieve because it is "not yet." We will realize in our hungry desire and our longing thirst that we are spiritually poor; for we will discover how far we are from true righteousness, from complete satisfaction. And we will crave it for others, we will seek it for all. We will know it as our greatest hope. This will include willing not only a sense of fairness to evolve in a world where the many have too little and the few have too much; but the universal love of God, obedience to God's kingdom, and a renewal within every heart of the image and likeness that exists in our human potential.

Righteousness is the likeness of God. Righteousness comes when we are set right with God, and right with the kingdom of God. Righteousness is Kingdom living. This beatitude is saying, "Blessed are those whose most intense desire is to enter into a right relationship with God." What is your heart's desire? Part of my heart's desire, as a pastor, is the righteousness of the congregation, the righteousness of the people I serve, as well as the righteousness needed in my community, in my whole world. It is a glorious goal, and will probably never be finally finished.

Goodness – Righteousness is one more thing – it is goodness. What if goodness had to be bought, and what if it's price was the cost of a meal, and you had to hunger and thirst for it? Where would it be in these modern times? How incredibly taken for granted it would become. It would seem forfeitable. And how desolate the world would be, because too few are really hungry enough, or, thirsty enough. Thank God, though, it's free. It's given to us abundantly. It's actually a part of our nature. it's within us like a spark just waiting to burst into flames

Goodness – Make it your vision. Make it your goal for yourself and for the world around you. Make it the subject of your daydreams; make it your fantasy. Through every individual goodness we can discover more than just something hoped for in some distant future. Make goodness a possibility. Make it a responsibility.

Too many good people are not hungry and thirsty enough. They don't seek any real righteousness. If they did the systematic sin and corruption of evils like pornography, promiscuity, drug abuse, gambling, violence, racism… and that unending list of social evils perpetuated by people lost and gone astray who claim their "right" to the pursuit of some wicked sense of happiness would have been crushed long ago. But good people aren't living up to the good they think they feel within themselves. Are you good? If so then what are you doing to stop the onslaught of all the evils and distortions of God's good gift of intimacy which systematically pervert the minds of both young and old all around you all the time. We're not even talking about the battles against such issues. We're detached. We feel good enough and that's enough for us.

But feel the hunger welling up inside you. Taste the dryness you sense in your thirst for goodness as you think about these issues. Feel it… for God's sake. Feel it for righteousness' sake. Feel it and crave for the goodness the world so desperately lacks. Jesus has promised that you will be satisfied.

Satisfaction – This beatitude is the key to the whole Sermon on the Mount. Jesus whole message is concerned with the state of *being* faithful much more than just *looking* faithful. It is concerned with the spirit of the law as much as the letter of the law. It is concerned with the inward witness as much as it is with the outward ritual. Faith must be internalized. We should keep rules because we believe in them, not just because we fear punishment. We should be righteous not only for what it will do for us, but for what our example can do for others. If only we revealed our hunger, our thirst for righteousness, maybe, just maybe, more people might crave eternal goodness instead of just what feels good in the instant.

And we're all thirsty. Before us lay an ocean of water. But we will soon learn that if we drink salt water, the thirst remains. It grows. We need to search inland for the pure spring that truly quenches our thirst. The salt water may look like the right stuff, but it's only the pure water that wells up from depths unplumbed that saves us. And there's a well, a fountain of life that's been uncovered and it's just waiting to be tapped. It's here in our midst; it's here in our fellowship; it's in the background of this Beatitude. It is there in the hymbook; it's here in the Bible. It's a kingdom and it's love. Blessed are those who hunger and thirst for righteousness. The curse is *not* wanting, *not* desiring, *not* searching for that something more. Tom Landry, the one time coach of the Dallas Cowboys, has said,

"The quality of a person's life is in direct proportion to their commitment to excellence." Commitment, hunger, thirst. Commitment to excellence, to goodness, to complete goodness, perfect goodness… It's commitment like this that satisfies.

Robert Louis Stevenson said that "To travel hopefully is better than to arrive." Hunger and thirst is as good as or better than the attainment of righteousness. And those who travel the road of commitment, and especially, commitment to Christ, travel hopefully. And, they arrive!

What's your greatest hunger? What's your greatest thirst? What's your greatest desire? What's the one thing you'd like to have more than anything else in the whole world? Is it righteousness? If so, you shall be satisfied! You are blessed.

THE JOURNEY HOME

"To travel hopefully is better than to arrive." So follow the directions.

I was lost once. The story is hilarious. It was my first time trick-or-treating on Halloween. I was with my older brother and several of his friends. After about five blocks away, I wanted us to cross the street and head back. My brother said, "Go ahead." So they left me (I was only 5), and I went in another direction. After trick-or-treating at three houses in what I thought was the right direction, nothing looked familiar. I had no idea where Robert was. The next house I came to, after ringing the doorbell, and having someone come to the door, with tears in my eyes, I said (instead of "Trick-or-Treat"), "I'm lost." I'm sure that must have been hilarious. But they let me in and very kindly asked me my name. When I told them I was Tommy Kingery, they knew exactly who I was, and, where I lived. "Is your father Buzz?" Yes! I explained that my big brother had left me to go my own way.

The home I happened to come to was the childhood home of Mary King, one of my father's old girlfriends!!! I told you this story was hilarious. Mary wasn't there, but her husband, Mr. Urban, was. He had brought his three kids to "Grandma's" house. One of the kids was Mike, who was my age.

Well, they happened to be about to leave anyway, and, very sympathetically, they let me get into their car and he drove me home.

Everything turned out fine, except for my brother, Robert. (That's another story!)

When we are lost, and we know it, like the Prodigal, we need sympathetic people who can help us find our way. We need directions, and, we need to follow them. One other thing, don't abandon your little brother on Halloween night!

Sometimes, what we need more than anything is good directions. I know it's a stereotypical image, but, how many wives have said, "Why don't you just stop and ask for directions?" Hilarious!

Dorothy was not in Kansas anymore, she was in Oz. She wanted to go home, but she had to see the Wizard. How did she find the Wizard? She had to "follow the yellow brick road!"

Follow directions. Lucky for Dorothy, she won the friendship of three helpful (?) companions. It's nice, when you are lost, to travel hopefully. But that happens best when you don't travel alone.

One last thing: Get good directions!

SCRIPTURES

To inspire a further consideration of an understanding of hunger and thirst, here are several relevant passages of Scripture:

John 6:35 – Jesus said to them, "I am the bread of life, whoever comes to me will never be hungry, and whoever believes in me will never be thirsty."

Deuteronomy 8:15 – Do not exalt yourself, forgetting the Lord your God who brought you out of the land of Egypt, out of the house of slavery, who led you through the great and terrible wilderness, an arid wasteland with poisonous snakes and scorpions. He made water flow for you from the flint rock, and fed you in the wilderness with manna that your ancestors did not know, to humble you and to test you, and in the end to do you good.

Nehemiah 9:15 – For their hunger you gave them bread from heaven, and for their thirst you brought water for them out of the rock, and you told them to go in to possess the land that you swore to give them.

Psalm 23:2b – He leads me besides still waters.

Psalm 34:10 – Young lions suffer want and hunger, but those who seek the Lord lack no good thing.

Psalm 63:1 – O God, you are my God, I seek you; my soul thirsts for you; my flesh faints for you, as in a dry and weary land where there is no water.

Psalm 78:15-16 – You split rocks open in the wilderness, and gave them drink abundantly as from the deep. He made streams come out of the rock, and caused waters to flow down like rivers.

Psalm 105:41 – He opened the rock and water gushed out; it flowed through the desert like a river.

Psalm 107:4-9 – Some wandered in desert wastes, finding no way to an inhabited town; hungry and thirsty, their soul fainted within them. Then they cried to the Lord in their trouble, and he delivered them from their distress; he led them by a straight way, and they reached an inhabited town. Let them thank the Lord for his steadfast love, for his wonderful for works to humankind. For he satisfies the thirsty, and the hungry he fills with good things.

Psalm 143:6 – I stretch out my hands to you; my soul thirsts for you like a parched land.

Proverbs 10:3 – The Lord does not let the righteous go hungry, but he thwarts the craving of the wicked.

Proverbs 16:26 – The appetite of workers works for them; they're hunger urges them on.

Isaiah 12:2-3 – Surely God is my salvation; I will trust and will not be afraid, for the Lord God is my strength and my might; he has become my salvation. With joy you will draw water from the wells of salvation.

Isaiah 49:10 – They shall not hunger or thirst, neither scorching wind nor sun shall strike them down, for he who has pity on them will lead them, and by springs of water will guide them.

Isaiah 55:1 – Ho, everyone who thirsts, come to the waters; and you that have no money, come, buy and eat. Come, buy wine and milk without money and without price.

Isaiah 58:11 – The Lord will guide you continually, and satisfy your needs in parched places, and make your bones strong; and you shall be like a watered garden, like a spring of water, whose waters never fail.

Amos 8:11 – The time is surely coming, says the Lord God, when I will send a famine on the land; not a famine of bread, or a thirst for water, but of hearing the words of the Lord.

Luke 1:53 – He has filled the Hungry with good things, and sent the rich away empty.

John 7:37-39 – On the last day of the festival, the great day, while Jesus was standing there, he cried out, "Let anyone who is thirsty come to me, and let the one who believes in me drink. As the scripture has said, 'Out of the believer's heart shall flow rivers of living water.'"

Philippians 4:12 – I know what it is to have little, and I know what it is to have plenty. In any and all circumstances I have learned the secret of being well fed and of going hungry, of having plenty and of being in need.

Revelation 7:16 – They will hunger no more, and thirst no more; the sun shall not strike them, nor any scorching heat.

Revelation 21:6-7 – Then he said to me, "It is done! I am the Alpha and the Omega, the beginning and the end. To the thirsty I will give water as a gift from the spring of the water of life.

Revelation 22:17 – Let everyone who is thirsty come. Let anyone who wishes take the water of life as a gift.

WHAT TO DO

Imagine some of the things in your life that make you happy. Make a quick list.

Bring happiness into the lives of others.

Ask yourselves, "How is happiness like wholeness?" Where does righteousness fit in?

Consider: "The moment we stop growing we start dying." How so? Is it always true?

Consider: "Earthly satisfactions are always only temporary." How is this true?

Feed your soul.

Read John 4:7-15. What is "living water"?

Consider: "Realize that hunger and thirst are a threat to life; so likewise the spiritually empty will perish eternally!" How is this true?

Learn and practice the true value of things

Think about some of the turning points in your life. What was happening?

Make goodness your vision.

Don't be detached. Seek righteousness in the world.

Consider: "Faith must be internalized." What does that mean?

A PRAYER

O Lord, You know our deepest needs and our truest desires: help us feel the true hunger within that sets us to searching for what is eternal. Inspire us to thirst for the truth that will help us to see, and, please, fill us with dreams of Your perfect Kingdom. And when we are hungry and thirsty for grace, please, give us a hope for what might fill our souls. This we ask in Jesus's great name. Amen.

A SONG

There Is a Hunger

There is a hunger, there is a thirst
     That can only finally be satisfied
When all is in order, and first things are first,
     And everything less is finally denied

     O come, let us drink from the well of God's blessing.
          Let our cups overflow with the peace of His Way.
     And let's all proclaim the faith we're confessing,
          For we bring the light of a glorious new day.

There is a longing, a burning desire
     That is always arising from deep in our soul.
It touches our hearts and it sets us on fire
     And awakens the mind by the Spirit's control.

     O come, let's ignite a new fire, a new vision.
          Let us strive for the glory that Truth only knows.
     And let's conquer the doubt of our weak indecision
          Let us follow God's blessing wherever it goes.

     Let us find strength in the joy of our dreams.
     And let us be channels for God's perfect streams.

CHAPTER FIVE

THE MERCIFUL

Blessed are the merciful,
for they will receive mercy.
Matthew 5:7

The Beatitudes – Having a sense of purpose is a good beginning. I have already spoken about how every life needs a sense of purpose. A sense of purpose brings life meaningfulness. But just having a purpose is not enough. We need to do something about that purpose. We need to figure out what can fulfill that purpose. Once we have that goal, the end, in mind, we need to discern a means to reach that end.

A "means" is a method for achieving an "end", or, goal. I was usually fairly good at helping the congregations I served develop goals. But the planning process needs to develop programs that will lead us to those goals. That's where I relied on the idea people for *programming*. If it was a project that was attached to a building program, for example, there were steps that needed to be taken to reach that goal. Estimates had to be made, we needed to know exactly what had to be done, and, we needed to know the cost. Fundraising was always a big first step. Before we started to do something big, we needed to be able to pay for it. Raising funds was always a necessary responsibility in my ministry. I can't believe how many projects were accomplished over the years. And I loved filling in the color on a thermometer chart.

We need to think about how to get there. And The Beatitudes are a sort of program. They are a means to the end of blessedness.

It is said that the Beatitudes comprise the several stages of the Christian journey. They are the successive steps which a Christian takes on the path of life with Christ. They are like stages in the "naturalization" process for citizenship in the kingdom of God. And in a way we are all spiritual immigrants voyaging toward a common goal: blessedness, or, happiness. Happiness is both our goal and our way of traveling. Happiness does not depend on things or possessions, but on how we look at them. To measure our happiness by certain conditions is wrong. We can't keep saying, "If only…" and then wait for happiness. Some might think that they can pursue happiness *after* they've reached a certain point in their life. And they say, "If only that or this could happen…" then they could be happy/ blessed. And, though that may be true in some circicumstances, happiness is as much an attitude as an experience; and attitudes are more important, sometimes, than circumstances. Robert Schuler even called the Beatitudes "the be-happy attitudes".

This inner attitude becomes clearer as we begin to talk about mercy and purity. John Wesley in his sermon on the Beatitudes reiterates the process by which faith unfolds in an individual. As he speaks on the pure of heart, he says that we are ultimately purified through faith in the Blood of Jesus. Through the power of His grace, the pure in heart are those who are purified from pride. By remorse over our sinfulness, by the deep sense of our poverty of spirit, we are enabled to plea for God's help. Remember, "Blessed are the poor in spirit, for theirs is the kingdom of God." The pure in heart are those who are purified from indifference and detachment; they feel the sadness of our human condition, they grieve in holy mournfulness. The pure in heart develop a purer compassion, a refined empathy. And Jesus said, "Blessed are those who mourn, for they shall be comforted." The pure in heart are those who are purified from anger and from every unkind or turbulent passion by virtue of their meekness and gentleness. "Blessed are the meek, for they shall inherit the earth." The pure in heart are purified from every desire but the desire to please and enjoy God, to know and love him more and more by their hunger and thirst for righteousness. "They shall be comforted." Such comfort now engrosses their whole soul so much so that, now, they "Love the Lord their God with all their heart, and with all their soul, and with all their strength, and with all their mind" (Luke 10:27). It is at this point, the point of love, where the pilgrim of faith begins to become the blessed merciful.

<u>Blessing</u> – Sometimes feeling relieved after a crisis or a danger is over can bring a smile to our faces. Mercy brings relief. It is a blessing to experience mercy. Mercy is receiving a pardon. It is release for the captive. It is comfort for the afflicted. How relieved we become when we hear from the doctor and they are able to tell us that the surgery was successful. Everyone related to the patient will have a smile on their face, and some will be crying tears of joy. It's like that when a baby is born, when mom and baby are both well. What a relief! The tension is over. Now recovery can begin. Mercy is a blessing. And those who offer mercy to others will be blessed because mercy is given to them.

<u>Blessed Are The Merciful</u> – John Wesley suggests that the more we are filled with the righteousness of God, the more tenderly we will be concerned for those who are still without God. Out of our tender-hearted compassion, we will so grieve for those who do not hunger and thirst for God, that we will want to serve their souls, we will want to seek for them the salvation that we have known. It is like the desire to defend the defenseless, to stand up for the accused and to help them find justice. We will want to "Do unto others what we would want others to do unto us" (Matthew 7:12); to "love our neighbors as ourselves" (Luke 10:27b).

In John Wesley's sermon he then unfolds the vast importance of love by recounting the beautiful passage from 1st Corinthians 13 (4-7), where "Love is patient and kind; love is not jealous or boastful; it is not arrogant or rude. Love does not insist on its own way; it is not irritable or resentful; it does not rejoice in wrong, but rejoices in the rightL Love bears all things, believes all things, hopes all things, endures all things."

With patience, love realizes that, perhaps, God is not finished with us yet. In its kindness, love overcomes evil with good. In it's lack of jealousy, love is not hasty to pass sentence; in it's lack of boastfulness, love honors others; and being neither arrogant nor rude, love Is never patronizing, nor is it ever willingly offensive but up-building, nice. By not insisting on its own way, love does not think of itself, but of others. Love does not have room for being irritable, but stands fast, unprovoked; and love does not rejoice at wrong, at mistakes or at errors in judgment. Love rejoices in what is right, in the truth, in the good. Love bears all things – it can resist the temptation to be judgmental and unmerciful. Love believes all things – even when proven to the contrary, love still looks for that spark of good will that is in all people. And finally, love endures all things – it can take abuse and not be crushed.

It is impossible to have thoughts of resentment and jealousy, anger, hate, or ill will, and feel blessed. You cannot sow these negative seeds and expect to raise a garden of happiness. Not if you are normal!

To John Wesley, the merciful have the love that's needed in order for us to place ourselves in another's position and know the care they lack. Mercy is a sympathetic appreciation of others that enables us to see their point of view, and feel with them. The Good Samaritan showed mercy. Jesus ends this teaching by saying, "Go and do likewise" (Luke 10:28). Mercy is that outgoing, far-reaching, and outward looking love that is the great characteristic of the relationships of Christians with their fellow human beings.

In a legal sense, mercy is the remission of a deserved penalty. It is to commute the sentence, to pardon the convicted, to offer clemency. To be merciful is to agree not to treat someone badly when they may, by worldly standards, deserve it. To agree to suspend judgment and offer care... this is mercy. In a world that seems callous and unsympathetic, mercy is more than emotional pity. It is more than just giving help. Mercy is identification with others. To be merciful is to express the Incarnation. God became human, identified with us, with his creation. Mercy is a part of God's likeness. Jesus Christ is the mercy of God sent "not to condemn the world but that the world might be saved through him" (John 3:17). We, too, need to carry on that Incarnation through sacrificial loving-kindness.

Kindness – The basic idea is kindness. Too often we live in a win-lose reality. If I win, you lose; or, if you win, I lose. To be merciful is to be in a win-win reality. You win, but I win too, because I serve your gain. I can rejoice at your redemption. Jesus even said that to gain your life you must lose it (Matthew 16:25). It's a win-win reality. To be merciful is to help another person win, but you win too, because the merciful shall obtain mercy! Someone once said that "the greatest virtue is to lessen the misery of others." This is the attitude of a Mother Teresa. She even said once, to Malcom Muggeridge, a reporter, who thought the joyful look on her face was a put on, that nothing makes you happier than when you really reach out in mercy to someone who is badly hurt. It's like doctors, they don't make themselves feel better, but they still win.

Kindness. This is the basis of God's relationship to humankind. "God delights in mercy" (Micah 7:18) "God's mercy reaches to the heavens" (Psalm 57:10). Mercy is God's steadfast love (Psalm 36:7). "How precious is thy steadfast love, O God. The children of men take refuge in thy wings. With thee is the fountain of life. In Thy light do we see light" (Psalm 36:7-9). In Psalm 136 it says 26 times that God's steadfast love endures forever. Without mercy, there is only Law. Without Mercy there is no trust. Mercy is connected with truth, fidelity, commitment, loyalty. Mercy is God's loyalty to those who are loyal to his purpose. Mercy is founded on the promise of God to be with us always. A world without God is a world without mercy; and a world without Mercy is a world without God.

They shall obtain mercy – The evil show no mercy. To a pagan world, where unwanted children or infirm adults were discarded, where the stoic mind was seen as virtuous, Christ proclaims the blessings of mercifulness. We are to be merciful with one another not only seven times but 70 times seven times (Matthew 18:21-22) Paul teaches that "we reap what we sow" (Galatians 6:7). Matthew 6:14-15 says, "If you forgive others their trespasses, your heavenly father will also forgive you; but if you do not forgive others their trespasses neither will your father forgive your trespasses." And Matthew 7:2 says, "With the judgment you pronounce, you will be judged; and the measure you give will be the measure you get."

The merciful are too aware of their own sins to condemn others. They are penitential through merciful deeds, having learned the truth in love, and then, "doing unto others as they would have others do unto them" (Matthew 7:12); so they obtain God's mercy. Mercy is something that is received when it is given. To be merciful is to think of others the way God does; to feel for them as God feels; and act toward others as God acts towards them. And God might even act through us! To be merciful is to let God work through us.

The one great requirement of God in Micah 6:8, is "to do justice, to love mercy, and to walk humbly with your God." "Once God has spoken, twice have I heard this: that power belongs to God. and to Thee, O Lord, belongs mercy. For thou doest repay to all according to their work" (Psalm 62:11-12).

A world without God is a world without mercy.

This is the beatitude with an attitude. It's the attitude that "goodness and mercy shall follow me all the days of my life" (Psalm 23:6). Mercifulness is a choice to react positively and hopefully in every negative situation. The Prodigal father chose to be merciful. If you want people to be good to you, be good to them; if you want people to be nice to you, be nice to them; if you want people to be merciful to you, be merciful to his other children, and God's care will carry you so you can then carry others

Robert Schuler says that the opposite of mercifulness is self-centeredness. Self-centeredness turns life into a burden. Unselfishness turns burdens into life. The best thing to do for our inner wounds is to live a life of mercy. Don't nurse your wounds. Don't curse your wounds. Don't rehearse your wounds. Immerse them in loving deeds of mercy, and in doing so, your wounds will reverse; your wounds will make you a more sensitive, compassionate, considerate, gracious, and merciful person.

The Journey Home – The Prodigal is hoping to receive mercy when he arrives home. Every step forward, in the right direction, is filled with hope. The Prodigal is a changed person. They have left the past behind. Does doubt sneak in now and then? Does he wonder about his father's mercy? His love? What about his brother? Does he imagine relief when they see him. He is sure they may think disappointing thoughts about what he bas done; where he has been.

But his look is a forward look; his thoughts about "home" are filling his thoughts with positive images. Anything will be better than what be has left behind. His goal, now, is a positive one. His purpose is no longer just "escape", it is safety, security, and it is hopeful.

I have known several people who have finished their sentence and done their time, who, on returning home felt mixed blessings. Depending on their crime, trust was sometimes hard to find. One of the greatest joys I have known was felt by a man whose release date had arrived. I was coming into the prison while he was on his way out. (I did my internship in the Federal Corrections Institute {a prison} in Englewood, Colorado.) He was overjoyed, relieved. He was mostly glad to be on his way out of there. But I'm sure he was looking forward to returning to a life that would bring new, and, more blessings. Either way, congratulations were in order. I told him I was proud that he was now able to truly go forward.

Mercy is very redeeming.

Scriptures

To inspire a further consideration of an understanding of mercy, here are several relevant passages of Scripture:

Matthew 9:13 – "Go and learn what this means, 'I desire mercy, and not sacrifice.' For I have come to call not the righteous but sinners."

1 Chronicles 16:34 – O give thanks to the Lord for he is good; his steadfast love endures forever.

Proverbs 28:13 – No one who conceals transgressions will prosper; but one who confesses and forsakes them will obtain mercy.

Psalm 130:1-2 – Out of the depths I cry to you, O Lord; Lord hear my voice. Let your ears be attentive to the voice of my supplications.

Isaiah 30:18 – Therefore the Lord waits to be gracious to you. Therefore he will rise up to show mercy to you. For the Lord is a God of justice; blessed are those who wait for him.

Isaiah 55:7 – Let the wicked forsake their way and the unrighteous their thoughts. Let them return to the Lord that he may have mercy on them, and to our God for he will abundantly pardon.

Lamentations 3:22-23 – The steadfast love of the Lord never ceases; his mercies never come to an end; they are new every morning. Great is your faithfulness.

Micah 7:18-19 – Who is a God like You, pardoning iniquity and passing over the transgressions of the remnant of your possession. He does not retain his anger forever because he delights to show them clemency.

Matthew 6:14-15 – For if you forgive others their trespasses, your heavenly Father will also forgive you; but if you do not forgive others, neither will your Father forgive your trespasses.

Luke 1:50 – His Mercy is for those who fear Him from generation to generation.

Luke 6:36 – Be merciful just as your Father is merciful.

Ephesians 2:4-5 – But God, who is rich in mercy, out of the great love with which he has loved us, even when we were dead through our trespasses, made us alive together with Christ. By grace you have been saved.

Colossians 3:13 – Bear with one another; and if anyone has a complaint against another, forgive each other. Just as the Lord has forgiven you, so you also must forgive.

Hebrews 4:16 – Let us therefore approach the throne of grace with boldness so that we may receive mercy and find grace to help in time of need.

James 2:13 – For judgment will be without mercy to anyone who has shown no mercy. Mercy triumphs over judgment.

1 Peter 1:3 – Blessed be the God and father of our Lord Jesus Christ; by his great mercy, he has given us a new birth into a living hope through the resurrection of Jesus Christ from the dead.

Titus 3:5 – He saved us, not because of any works of righteousness that we have done, but according to his Mercy.

WHAT TO DO

Be merciful. Never seek revenge!

Be forgiving. Hold nothing against another.

Be patient… with yourself, and with others.

Think about what you are doing that will lead you to your goals.

Consider this sentence: "The Beatitudes are like stages in the "naturalization" process for citizenship in the kingdom of God." How so?

Consider this: "Happiness does not depend on things or possessions, but on how we look at them." Is this always true? How so?

Another sentence to consider: Happiness is as much an attitude as an experience; and attitudes are more important, sometimes, than circumstances... Do you agree?

Reflect: Mercy is receiving a pardon. It is release for the captive. It is comfort for the afflicted... How?

Consider: "You cannot sow negative seeds and expect to raise a garden of happiness."

What does this mean?

Consider: 'I desire mercy, and not sacrifice.' What does this mean?

Think: How does mercy triumph over judgment?

James 2:13 says, "For judgment will be without mercy to anyone who has shown no mercy. Mercy triumphs over judgment." Show mercy to others so that, at a minimum, you will be shown mercy from God.

A Prayer

O Lord, You are merciful, even when we don't deserve it. May faith be freedom from captivity, from guilt, from sin. Change us by Your love, and set us on the path of righteousness and grace. Give us the patience we need to be merciful toward others, and the strength to offer forgivness 70 times 7 times. May Your mercies never come to an end. We ask this prayer in Jesus's name. Amen.

A Poem

Lord, Have Mercy

Lord have mercy, for I have sinned.
I set my sails against Your wind
And deviated from my course,
losing touch with the true source
That could have shown a better way.
And that's what's brought me to this day.

Forgive me for my many faults,
My foolishness and my assaults
On truth and goodness, on what is right,
On beauty, love, and on Your Light.

There are heights I might have known,
If I had thought the seeds I'd sown
Would have produced the wicked fruits
That I have plucked up by the roots.
O God, help me remember that I've found
That Your mercy and Your love abound.

CHAPTER SIX

THE PURE IN HEART

Blessed are the pure in heart,
for they will see God.
Matthew 5:8

The Beatitudes – A vision of the goal can encourage us to move in that direction. How clear are your goals? How enticing are they? Do they draw you to them? Do feel compelled? How will you know when you've reached your destination?

A Marathon runner keeps the finish line in mind even as they keep their eyes on the immediate steps ahead. Not wanting to lose control, they are very careful about where they step. But the finish line is their vision, their goal.

The first time I went skiing, I was in Grenoble, France. The ski lift to the top of our mountain was a good seven or eight minute ride. After so long, I looked back. We could no longer even see the bottom of the slope. The hills I had to ski over had consumed the goal. Long story short, I virtually fell down the mountain. A hundred yards or so staying upright, and then I would fall. I was told not to worry about the bottom, "Just focus on where you want to go next." Of course, I needed to realize that my goal was not just the bottom of the slope. My goal included just being on the mountain skiing (falling too). It was glorious.

Even when we can't see the actual destination, we can see the next mile ahead. And then, the next, and the next… Achieving some distance is better than going nowhere. I have already spoken of how the Beatitudes are steps toward blessedness. And while blessedness may seem far ahead, every step in that direction is a blessing. After all, we are walking the road of promise.

Blessing – A promise begins now and goes on forever. I didn't promise to take Carol to be my wife just for the honeymoon, my promise was until death parted us! When we begin to feel blessed because our journey is taking us somewhere, toward some goal, the promise of arriving at our destination has many moments of joy, happiness. Meanwhile, we enjoy the journey. You don't think about the end of the promise. In marriage, you are in the promise. And the promise is in you.

Jesus makes several promises to His followers as He tells them the Beatitudes. The blessing begins even before the promise is fulfilled. We don't have to be completely pure before we can have a vision of God. In the scriptures, every encounter with God by those called to be faithful was with someone far from perfect. We don't need to acquire a certain amount of insight before we can become insightful. You don't need to know the whole truth before you can tell the truth you know. Don't wait for happiness to be a part of your journey simply because you believe you can be even happier. Don't wait to bless others with mercy because you haven't received all the mercy you hoped for. Just be blessed, and, be a blessing!

The Pure in Heart – In effect, mercy is what purifies us. "Blessed are the pure in heart, for they shall see God!" This proclamation goes beyond ritualistic regulations. There were 132 physical blemishes laid down in the Law that could disqualify a man from the Hebrew priesthood – those who could enter the holiest of Holies in the Temple, to "see" God. But the heart is not mentioned on tbe list. Jesus looks beyond the outward ritualisti requirements, where, on the surface, one could *look* pure, but He encourages looking to the inward virtues. Purity of heart implies a type of lifestyle, and, a state of mind. Jesus is thinking of more than just not being dirty or polluted. He is not referring to our use of language, but the righteousmess connected with those things came naturally with purity of heart. Jesus is actually getting to the *heart* of the matter,

By "heart" is meant thoughts, desires, motives, attitudes – the whole personality or inner person. Jesus has said that "Where your treasure is, there will your heart be also" (Matthew 6:21). If your treasure is clean, unmixed, and single – as in pure gold – your heart will be clean, unmixed, and single. If you aim at too many treasures, your heart will be a mass of confusion.

Later in Matthew, Jesus proclaims the woefulness of the Pharisees in their hypocrisy as they "cleanse the outside of the cup and of the plate, but inside they are full of greed and self-indulgence." He says, "First clean the inside… that the outside also may be clean" (Matthew 23:25-26).

Toward the end of His Sermon on the Mount, he tells the disciples to "enter by the narrow gate; for the gate is wide and the way is easy that leads to destruction, and those who enter by it are many. For the gate is narrow and the way is hard that leads to life, and those who find it are few" (Matthew 7:13-14).

Jesus says that "a sound tree cannot bear evil fruit, nor can a bad tree bear good fruit" (Matthew 7:18). He's talking about the inward witness, the inner being. This is what deteremines tbe trutb of our status before God! Jesus would not want us to lead an unexamined life. We must ask God, "Create in me a clean heart, and put a new and right spirit in me" (Psalm 51:10). And Jesus concludes His illustration about bearing fruit by saying, "You will know them by their fruits" (Matthew 7:20).

A promise proclaimed by Jeremiah is that God will write his law upon our hearts and make the law a part of who we really are; "and no longer shall each man teach his neighbor and each his brother saying, 'Know the Lord,' for they will all know me…and I will remember their sin no more" (Jeremiah 31:33-34). It sounds like they will also receive mercy!

God's promise in Ezekiel is heard in these words: "I will sprinkle clean water upon you, and you shall be clean,,, A new heart I will give you, and a new spirit will I put within you; and I will take out of your flesh the heart of stone, and give you a heart of flesh. And I will put my Spirit within you… And I will deliver you…" (Ezekiel 36:25-29). Again purity of heart is revealed through God's mercy!

God is pure – holy! Holiness is sanctification. And John Wesley proclaimed very strongly the belief in Sanctifying Grace. It is the grace that continues to work in us after we have been justified, changed; after we have begun to believe, repented, and begun a right relationship with God.

Sanctifying Grace is known more commonly as the grace that inspires spiritual growth – growing deeper, closer, more godly. We may never be completely sanctified, or, perfected, or purified in this life, but we can sometimes feel very close. And ohhh, wat a wonderfdul grace it is.

Think, for a moment, though, about how purity is scoffed at. Purity has often been promoted rather superficially. It is for Catholic priests and nuns. We think purity is something that can only be pursued by a lifetime of effort, dedication, and commitment. It's because we imagine purity as perfect innocence, complete freedom of guilt. It is, but isn't that the kingdom of heaven? We're not there yet either, but we don't scoff at the prospect of arriving in heaven in our future. We sometimes imagine purity as a vision of consuming judgment, where grain is winnowed from the chaff, and the chaff is burned with fire (Matthew 3:12). Yes, but, God is not done working on us, or in us, and we need to let the Potter shape us. God isn't finished with any of us yet. And, yes, it's all right to mix my metaphors!

So purity can actually be something a little more within our sight. Perhaps in includes having more of a clear conscience, having a single direction, unmixed motives. Soren Kierkegaard published a treatise entitled Purity of Heart Is to Will One Thing. Purity of heart is a sincerity of purpose. Too often we aim for the impressive instead of the true. And, though what is true can be very impressive, what impresses people is not always what is true. And too often we suffer from the "rewards" syndrome where we desire something for the sake of the rewards we think we will receive, rather than for the truth's sake. Purity includes the sincerity of single-mindedness, willing one thing, hungering for it, thirsting for it. We are impure when we are insincere, double-minded, acting with mixred motives

Our double-mindedness is condemned by Jesus as he proclaims the fulfillment of the Law with His life. It's not only "You shall not kill," but, "You shall not be angry" (Matthew 5:21, 22). Adultery is a sin, but so is thinking about it in your heart. Jesus says, "If your right eye causes you to sin, pluck it out… If your right hand causes you to sin, cut it off… It is better to lose a part of your outward self, than to lose your whole self" (Matthew 5:17, 21-23, 29-30 My paraphrase). Jesus says, "Let what you say be simply 'yes' or 'no', anything more than this comes from evil" (Matthew 5:37). Purity is this sort of singleness of mind. It has no confusion, no double standards, no mixed motives. No compromises. It is focussed. Too often we compromise our faith simply by blurring our vision with desires that fall short of God's will, God's Truth, and God's purity.

They Shall See God – Having to keep our eyes on more than one master at once, makes us cross-eyed. Our vision goes out of focus. Neither master is clearly seen. But the eyes of the pure in heart are single, focussed on one thing. Their sight is unimpaired and undistracted. By having our true goals in focus, we can better concentrate on the road ahead, and, on the truth of the subject in our vision.

Do you see God when you look at your heart? When you look *with* your heart? God is there. Do you see God when you look at the hearts of others? God is there as well. What impedes your vision of God? Do you *have* a vision of God? Seek the Lord while He may be found!

Realize that what we see often depends on more than what our eyes perceive. Perspective happens sometimes, by virtue of *how* we look at things; on what we *want* to see. For the average person, to look at the sky at night, there's only a mass of stars, and they may look beautifdul. But to an astronomer, the stars become a map, a source for navigation and direction.

Striving for purity of heart can give us a whole new way of looking at things. When there are no conflicting loyalties, no mixed hypocritical intentions, then there is a greater determination. Perhaps we will begin to see things as God sees them, as an extension of His creativity, the way a potter can be known by their pots.

Other people will be seen as God's likeness. When King Saul had lost the Holy Spirit due to his disobedience and resentments, and Samuel came to anoint God's new chosen ruler, God told Samuel, "The Lord sees not as a human sees; humans look on the outward appearance, but the Lord looks upon the heart" (1 Samuel 16:7). We must, therefore, regard no one from a human point of view (2 Corinthians 5:16).

The more we become pure in beart, the more we will begin to look upon God's creation and see the trace of His touch. Rain can be seen as God's cleansing. Flowers can be seen as God's smile. Wind can be thought of as God's whisper. Stones can be seen as God's power. People can be thought of as God's servants. Everything becomes an agent of God's grace.

We can see each other as God's gifts given to each other. Everything can begin to reveal God.

When we become pure in heart, we will have a purer system of values. By willing only One Thing, our wills become God's will. We can let God work in us and through us, and we'll feel it. We will see ourselves differently. "For now we see in a mirror dimly. But then, face to face" (1 Corinthians 13:12a). Purity. Vision. Mercy. Love. You see, the vision of mercy is a vision of God's loving nature. The experience of divine love is like seeing God. Blessed are the pure in heart, for they shall see God! Who wouldn't want to have vision like this?

Paul said it well: "I want to know Christ and the power of His Resurrection and the sharing of His sufferings by becoming like him in his death, if somehow, I may attain the resurrection of the dead. Not that I have already obtained this, or, have already reached the goal; but I press on to mke it my own, because Christ Jesus has made me His own. Beloved, I do not consider that I have made it my own, but this one thing I do: forgetting what lies behind and straining forward to what lies ahead, I press on toward the goal for the prize of the heavenly call of God in Christ Jesus" (Philippians 3:10-14).

John Wesley called it "Striving nfor Perfection". Pressing on toward the goal, becoming pure in heart!

The Journey Home – The Prodigal is on his way. He presses on! The further he gets from what he's left behind, the more he feels blessed because of where he's going. After surgery, I felt weak. I needed to rest and recuperate, but I also needed to rebuild my strength. It wasn't too hard because it was very easy to see myself several days from now, several weeks from now, even months. It's been almost two years, and though I'm nowhere near what I used to be years ago (Who is?), I can walk fairly well (though I limp), and, I can now swim a mile at a time. I could be doing a lot worse. I may not be where I want to be, yet; but I can still be productive. This is my 15th book!

The Prodigal sees a future so much better than what his "now" had become. In fact, his "now' is already different. It is miles better. He knows he's not home, but the singularity of his vision has him laser-focussed on getting there. His plan: just let me be a hired man in your service, father. I'll see you soon.

SCRIPTURES

To inspire a further consideration of an understanding of purity of heart, here are several relevant passages of Scripture:

Psalm 19:9 – The fear of the Lord is pure, enduring forever.

Psalm 24:3-4 – Who shall ascend the hill of the Lord? And who shall stand in his holy place? Those who have clean hands and pure hearts, who do not lift up their souls to what is false, and do not swear deceitfully.

Psalm 51:6-7 – You desire truth in the inward being; therefore teach me wisdom in my secret heart. Purge me with hyssop, and I shall be clean; wash me, and I shall be whiter than snow.

Psalm 51:10 – Create in me a clean heart, O God, and put a new and right spirit within me.

Psalm 119:9 – How can young people keep their way pure? By guarding it according to your word.

Proverbs 16:2 – All one's ways may be pure in one's own eyes, but the Lord weighs the spirit.

Proverbs 22:11 – Those who love a pure heart, and are gracious in speech, will have the king as a friend.

Luke 11:34-35 – Your eye is the lamp of your body. If your eye is healthy, your whole body is full of light; but if it is not healthy, your body is full of darkness. Therefore consider whether the light in you is not darkness.

1 Corinthians 6:13 – The body is meant not for fornication but for the Lord, and the Lord for the body.

2 Corinthians 6:4-7 – We have commended ourselves in every way: through great endurance, in afflictions, hardships, calamities, beatings,

imprisonments, riots, labors, sleepless nights, hunger; by purity, knowledge, patience, kindness, holiness of spirit, genuine love, truthful speech, and the power of God; with the weapons of righteousness for the right hand and for the left; in honor and dishonor, in ill repute and good repute.

Philippians 1:9-11 – This is my prayer: that your love may overflow more and more with knowledge and full insight to help you to determine what is best, so that in the day of Christ you may be pure and blameless, having produced the harvest of righteousness that comes through Jesus Christ for the glory and praise of God.

Philippians 2:14-15 – Do all things without murmuring and arguing, so that you may be blameless and innocent, children of God without blemish in the midst of a crooked and perverse generation, in which you shine like stars in the world.

Philippians 4:8 – Think about whatever is pure.

Colossians 3:5 – Put to death, therefore, whatever in you is earthly: fornication, impurity, passion, evil desire, and greed (which is idolatry).

1 Thessalonians 4:7 – God did not call us to impurity but in holiness.

1 Timothy 4:12 – Let no one despise your youth, but set the believers an example in speech and conduct, in love, in faith, in purity.

1 Timothy 5:22b – Keep yourself pure.

Hebrews 9:14 – How much more will the blood of Christ, who through the eternal Spirit offered himself without blemish to God, purify our conscience from dead works to worship the living God!

Hebrews 12:14 – Pursue peace with everyone, and the holiness without which no one will see the Lord.

James 1:27 – Religion that is pure and undefiled before God, the

Father, is this: to care for orphans and widows in their distress, and to keep oneself unstained by the world.

James 4:8 – Draw near to God, and he will draw near to you. Cleanse your hands, you sinners, and purify your hearts, you double minded.

1 Peter 1:15-16 – As he who called you is holy, be holy yourselves in all your conduct; for it is written, "You shall be holy for I am holy".

1 Peter 1:22 – Now that you have purified your souls by your obedience to the truth so that you have genuine mutual love, love one another deeply from the heart.

1 John 1:9 – If we confess our sins, he was faithful and just will forgive us our sins and cleanse us from all unrighteousness.

WHAT TO DO

Seek purity, and, practice it!

Ask yourself: How clear are your goals?

Consider this sentence: "Achieving some distance toward the goal is better than going nowhere." Do you agree? How is this true?

Consider: "The promise of arriving at our destination has many moments of joy." The journey is not always easy and the promise of arriving doesn't alays seem present, but …go forward!

Consider this sentence: "We don't have to be completely pure before we can have a vision of God." Try to see what God wants to show you.

"We don't need to acquire a certain amount of insight before we can become insightful. You don't need to know the whole truth before you can tell the truth you know." Remind yourself that you have insights and truth to share!

"Jesus looks beyond the outward ritualistic requirements, where, on the surface, one could *look* pure, but He encourages looking to the inward virtues." Look beyond the surface!

Think about your treasures. What are they. Make a list.

Think: What does Jesus mean by saying, "You will know them by their fruits" (Matthew 7:20).

Think: What does Ezekiel mean when he mentions receiving "a new heart"?

Let the Potter shape you. What does that mean?

Consider this sentence: "Purity includes the sincerity of single-mindedness, willing one thing, hungering for it, thirsting for it." Are you sincere? Are you hungry?

Consider: "Realize that what we see often depends on more than what our eyes perceive. Perspective happens sometimes, by virtue of *how* we look at things; on what we *want* to see." What do you *want* to see?

"The Lord sees not as a human sees; humans look on the outward appearance, but the Lord looks upon the heart" (1 Samuel 16:7). Look on the heart!

"The further rhe Prodigal gets from what he's left behind, the more he feels blessed because of where he's going." How has this been true in your life?

Confess your sins. It will cfleanse you from unrighteousness.

A PRAYER

Almighty God, purify my heart. I am nowhere near the purity I should experience, but I want to get there. Help me to press on toward the goal. Help me to take steps toward perfection; even small steps, day by day. May I receive singleness of heart. Help me to be sincere. And guide me in the way I need to go. This I ask in Jesus's name. Amen.

A POEM

Give Me A Vision

God, give me a vision; let it be clear.
Inspire my spirit, let me draw near.
Let me be glad that the past is the past,
And set my heart free from the woes I've amassed.
God, give me the strength to arrive at my goal
Where beauty awaits to be poured on my soul.

You have given a taste of Your Kingdom of bliss.
I believe that, in heaven, it's something like this:
The power of evil is defeated and done,
And Jesus has conquered – Your triumphant Son! –
Pain is replaced with both comfort and joy
And blessings abound in the peace You deploy.

Ignite in my conscience the fire of what's true
And make it bring light upon all that I do.
  And let me be happy; and let me be blessed.
  O Lord, let me enter Your wonderful rest.

CHAPTER SEVEN

THE PEACEMAKERS

Blessed are the peacemakers,
for they will be called the children of God.
Matthew 5:9

How do you fight for peace? Begin with surrender!

<u>The Beatitudes</u> – Recipes take some degree of understanding before you try to use them to bake or cook. For example, you have to know what a *tsp* is! Then you have to accurately (?) follow the steps in preparation. Have you ever baked nothing for 20 minutes before you realized the oven wasn't even turned on? Mine beeps when the temperature I've set has arrived. Then I can put what I'm making in the oven.

The Beatitudes are a recipe for peace. They help us understand the ingredients needed in the journey of faith; how to apply them, and what to do. The difference with the Beatitudes is that you can begin to be a peacemaker even when you are mournful, or thirsty….even before you are complerely righteous!

By following a recipe, and preparing everything, then comes a time for patience. Most of the time, cooking something takes… time. But when you can smell that pie in the oven, it makes you want to eat it even before is is "done". But a recipe includes a promise. The promise begins to be fulfilled when the baking is done. Stay patient, though, just taking the pie out of the oven does not mean it is ready to eat!

Blessing – Have you ever felt bad because you made a promise you just couldn't fulfill. Promises are hard, sometimes. Sometimes, "See you again" can't happen in our mortal lifetimes. But we believe we will see one another again when we all get to heaven. It will be a glorious reunion.

The beatitudes make promises almost too good to be true. When you feel humbled, it may seem impossible to believe in the promise that the Kingdom of Heaven will be yours. When you are weighed down with grief, it may seem impossible that comfort will come. When you are meek, it may be far-fetched to imagine inheriting the earth. Things may seem a bit more likely when you hunger and thirst for righteousness, and you are promised fulfillment. And being merciful can be its own reward, and that's exacrly what is promised. When we are called to be pure in heart, the promise is seeing God! Are you kidding? It seems way too good to be true. But when Christ makes these promises our hopes are lifted very high.

Hopes and promises are very neatly connected. Blessings are promised! Catch the blessing!

The Peacemakers – There is a peace that is an absence of war, the absence of destruction, the absence of violence, the absence of killing, the absence of conflict. But the absence of these things doesn't automatically create the presence of peace. Such absences are usually called a truce, a treaty. A good friend of mine told me about the cessation of fighting in Viet Nam for the holiday of Christmas one year. It was quiet in an eerie sort of way. There was nowhere to go, no preparations to make, no fighting to fear… for that one day. But one of his comrades said to him, "This kind of peace is scary."

The land around them was devastated; villages were in ruin, the local people were homeless, hungry, and diseased. In spite of the fact that there was an interlude of no fighting in the conflict, the conflict still existed. It was only a brief truce, and for many of the young men, it lasted too long, because it lasted long enough to let them cry. They cried for what had happened up to that truce, and they cried for what would happen when the truce was over. And they knew the truce would be over too soon.

The Conflict still existed! The peace was not real. It was scary. Scary, because the tensions were still high; because trouble still lay ahead; because it was still war. Once upon a time, we believed war made heroes. But I think we've learned… War means body-bags. War means arms, legs, and faces maimed and distorted. War means that something is not right with the world.

The United Methodist Social Principles on War and Peace, states in Paragraph VI. C (1984) – *We believe war is incompatible with the teachings and example of Christ. We therefore reject war as an instrument of national foreign policy and insist that the first moral duty of all nations is to resolve by peaceful means every dispute that arises between or among them; that human values must outweigh military claims as governments determine their priorities; that the militarism of society must be challenged and stopped; that the manufacture, sale, and deployment of armaments must be reduced and controlled; and that the production, possession, or use of nuclear weapons be condemned.*

The United Methodist Church believes in peace with justice! There is no peace if there is no justice.

Blessed are the peacemakers, for they shall be called children of God!

Conflict, tension, threats, and trouble are unjust. These things don't only exist in times of war. There are conflicts all around us, and, within us. They exist in families, in communities, in our nations, and in our hearts. Everywhere we look, unless we turn away and try to ignore it, there is trouble. People live in tension all the time. Threats of violence are vey real for too many people.

The Hebrew word for <u>peace</u> is *shalom*. The Greek word in the New Testament for *shalom* is *eirene*. It's where we get the name "Irene". Shalom/eirene in their fullest sense means wholeness, well-being, health. It includes prosperity, welfare, and security. But, in each sense, it always implies a relationship, a right relationship with self, with God, and with others.

<u>Peace Within</u> – Inner peace is the first effect of purity of heart. *Blessed are the pure in heart, for they shall see God.* Because of inner confusion, however, and a lack of focus and consistency, our inner tensions make us all walking civil wars, Because he felt moments when his heart was less than pure, even Paul said in Romans 7:19: "I know that nothing good dwells within me. I can will what is right, but I cannot do it. For I do not do the good I want, but the evil I do not want to do."

It's said that you can't be happy if you don't like yourself. In a way, that's not entirely true...if ignorance is bliss. Not knowing the inner confusion, or, by simply ignoring it, some people aren't aware of the inner tensions and conflicts that exist. But I don't believe such people can really know true happiness. An unexamined life does not deal with the very real problems that exist, so such people can never know the blessing of finding a sense of inner peace, a sense of focus, a sense of security. I would rather say that you just can't be happy if you cannot accept yourself, And acceptance is the first part of inner peace.

Studdert Kennedy published a poem that describes the feelings of a soldier in the First World War:

> Our padre says I'm a sinner, and John Bull says I'm a saint.
> And they're both of them bound to be liars, for I'm neither of them, I ain't.
> I'm a man and a man's a mixture, right down from his very birth.
> For part of him comes from heaven, and part of him comes from earth.
> There's nothing in him that is perfect, there's nothing that's all complete.
> He is no' but a great beginning from his head to the soles of his feet.

"Nothing but a great beginning!" I like that. William Barclay describes humankind as "part ape and part angel." We're a mixture. Peace comes in sorting things out... and putting them in the right order. So, in a way, we are all peacemakers trying to make peace with ourselves, trying to find an angel; to be what we'll become; trying to find an inner wholeness, an inner well-being, an inner health, a sense of order, and a sense of self-control.

Blessed are the peacemakers, for they shall be called children of God.

Peace With God – Peace within is connected to peace with God. We can't really be right with ourselves, or with anyone else, for that matter, until we can be right with God. This peace with God is the foundation of right relationships. Peace is living in harmony with God's plan. Righteous obedience gives us peace. Psalm 119:165 says, "Those who love thy law have great peace." Isaiah 26:3 says, "Thou wilt keep him in perfect peace whose mind is stayed on Thee." Perfect peace! And Isaiah 32:17 says,

"The effect of righteousness will be peace, and the result of righteousness, quietness and rest forever."

Peace includes a reconciliation, a returning to a right relationship with God. In Colossians 1:20 we are told that "through Jesus, God has reconciled all things to himself, making peace by the blood of the cross!" And in Philippians 4:7 it says, "The peace of God, which passes all understanding, will keep your hearts and your minds in Christ Jesus." And in Colossians 3:5, Paul said, "Let the peace of Christ rule in your hearts."

Let there be peace. Peace is there just waiting for us to let it happen. It happens because of the love that binds everything together in perfect harmony. God loves me, and that's enough to give me peace; the peace of security, the peace of tranquility, of wholeness, of well-being. God loves me…And God loves you! The only thing that prevents us from living together in perfect harmony is the barriers we hold in place. We need to break down those barriers and be able to say: God loves you, and so do I!

Peacemakers are barrier breakers!

Peace With Others – What are those barriers? What is it that keeps us from loving relationships? It's got to be more than race, gender, age, or language. We've experienced over and over how those walls keep tumbling down. And there is still a battle between the reconciling influences we believe in and the disruptive influences we have failed to defeat completely.

In a way, it all returns to our poverty of spirit and the lack of inner peace. When we can't accept ourselves, when we feel insecure about ourselves, we project our own inner tensions on to others. We carry a bundle of emotional baggage that often leaves us angry, frustrated, begrudging and bitter. But in our fallen, self-righteous ways, we think it is the other who is wrong, not us. So we refuse to try to understand each other. Our anxieties and insecurities are revealed in our inability to be truly reconciled to each other. And, more often than not, we live in a state of an uneasy truce rather than a state of peace. A truce may be nice; it may even feel good, but we'll never quite make it to the peace that brings the full blessing of being children of God. Sometimes, the truce itself can be the barrier.

They Shall Be Called the Children of God – It is the peacemakers that are blessed and called the children of God. It's not peace lovers, or peace hopers, or even peace prayers, but *makers*, builders. Unless we work for understanding; unless we strive for reconciliation; unless we work for real changes… in our lives, in our families, in our communities, and between nations… unless we struggle to resolve our conflicts and fashion a peacefulness that overcomes our confusions, striking at the roots of the problems, instead of just proclaiming truce after truce; unless we do this, we'll never know peace as God planned it! We need to cure the disease instead of merely salving the symptoms.

There are a lot of troublemakers all around us. And, in order for us to let the peace of Christ rule in our hearts, we can't let the troublemakers plant the seeds of conflict that might take root. God relieves us of this. We no longer feel like victims, but victors! The ultimate work of peacemaking is in reconciling others with God; for as long as people are at odds with God, they are at odds with themselves, and with their neighbors. Jesus is the Prince of Peace. Peacemaking is what God has done through Christ. God's kingdom is a Kingdom of peace. Christ is the reconciliation of God. And to be a peacemaker is to reflect the image of God the way Jesus did.

They shall be called children of God! And we are already children of God! God is our Father in heaven. We are created with this special relationship already among us, within us. But to be a real child of God includes recognizing all people as our brothers and sisters. Then peace becomes a power among us; the power to build up, the power to heal; because "I am a child of God!" What is there that we cannot do? Children… brothers and sisters…let's make peace!

I want to conclude the message of this chapter with a story. Back in the early 1940s, the fields of two ranchers shared the same border. One summer, when the rain was scarce, good grazing land became hard to find, and the cattle wandered back and forth across the open fields as they always had. Out of their frustration, each rancher blamed the other for using up each other's grazing land. Friends became feuders. One day, one of the angry ranchers went out and dug a trench along his side of the border. When the other rancher saw it, he came out and dug a trench along the border on his side. Then the first rancher came out and dug a deeper trench, a wider trench. Well, pretty soon they had a great impassable ditch.

It so happened that, right about that time, a stranger stopped at the house of the first rancher, looking for work. The rancher said, "Yes, build a fence along that ditch!" At the end of the day, the rancher went out to see how the job was going. He was shocked! Instead of a fence, the stranger had built a bridge. He had also opened up a trench by a nearby creek, and water was already pouring through the ditch, connecting downstream with a river.

He was about to get angry at the stranger when he suddenly heard tbe other rancher call out, smiling as he came across the bridge with his hand out. "What made you think of that idea? This is fantastic! With a little creek coming through here, our fields will never run dry!" As they continued to apologize and compliment each other, they didn't notice the stranger walking off. The first rancher finally turned to thank him, but noticing that he was leaving, he called out, "Hey! I've got a lot more work for you to do!" The stranger called back, "Yeah, but I've got a lot more bridges to build!"

Peace!

The Journey Home – Sometimes I wonder about the eagerness of the Prodigal as he journeys home. Is he hurrying? I imagine so. I imagine all the things he wants to do to "make up" for his bad choices, his offenses. How much will they matter? How will his faults be held against him? Reconciling with those we have offended might be difficult and awkward. This could make the Prodigal a bit anxious, even hesitant. Does he second-guess his decision to go to his father?

Life is rife with moments of second-guessing. If we have failed before, we might worry that we'll fail again. Stop the negative self-talk. Think poritively, optimistically. Hope can make everyone an optimist. We should like our goals. When we do, the steps toward them feel right, good. There may be persecution ahead. We may be doubted, hard to trust. But I'll talk about that in a few more chapters.

For now, think "peace". Peacemaking.

SCRIPTURES

To inspire a further consideration of an understanding of peace, here are several relevant passages of Scripture:

Psalm 4:8 – I will both lie down and sleep in peace; for you alone, O Lord, Make me lie down in safety.

Psalm 29:11 – May the Lord give strength to his people! May the Lord bless his people with peace!

Psalm 119:165 – Great peace have those who love your law; nothing can make them stumble.

Proverbs 3:16-18 – Long life is in her right hand, in her left are riches and honor. Her ways are ways of pleasantness, and all her paths are peace.. She is a tree of life to those who lay hold of her; those who hold her fast are called happy.

Isaiah 9:6 – …a child has been born for us the sun is given to us; …and his name shall be called Prince of Peace.

Isaiah 32:17 – the effect of righteousness will be peace, and the result of righteousness, quietness and trust forever.

Isaiah 52:7 – How beautiful upon the mountains are the feet of the messenger who announces peace, who brings good news, who announces salvation, who says to Zion, "Your god reigns."

Isaiah 53:5c – Upon him was the punishment that made us whole.

Isaiah 55:12 – For you shall go out in joy, and be led back in peace; the mountains and the hills before you shall burst into song, and all the trees of the field will clap their hands.

John 14:27 – Peace I leave with you; my peace I give to you. I do not give to you as the world gives. Do not let your hearts be troubled, and do not let them be afraid

John 16:33 – "I have said this to you so that in me you may have peace. In the world you face persecution. But take courage; I have conquered the world."

Romans 5:1 – Therefore since we are justified by faith, we have peace with God through our Lord Jesus Christ.

Romans 8:6b – To set the mind on the spirit is life and peace.

Romans 12:18 – …if it is possible, so far as it depends on you, live peaceably with all.

Romans 14:17 – The kingdom of God is not food and drink but righteousness and peace and joy in the Holy Spirit.

Romans 15:13 – May the god of Hope fill you with all joy and peace and believing, so that you may abound in Hope by the power of the Holy Spirit.

1 Corinthians 14:33 – God is a God not a disorder but of peace.

2 Corinthians 13:11 – Finally, brothers and sisters, farewell. Put things in order, listen to my appeal, agree, live in peace. And the God of love and peace will be with you.

Galatians 5:22 – The fruit of the spirit is …peace…

Ephesians 2:14 – For he is our peace; in his flesh he has made both groups into one and has broken down the dividing wall, that is, the hostility between us.

Philippians 4:6-7 – Do not worry about anything, but in everything by prayer and supplication, with thanksgiving, let your requests be made known to God. And the peace of God, which surpasses all understanding, will guard your hearts and your minds in Christ Jesus.

Philippians 4:9 – Keep on doing the things that you have learned and received and heard and seen in me, and the God of Peace will be with you.

Colossians 3:14-15 – Above all, clothe yourselves with love, which binds everything together in perfect harmony. And Let the peace of Christ rule in your hearts, to which indeed you were called in the one body. And be thankful.

2 Thessalonians 3:16 – Now may the Lord of peace himself give you peace at all times and always. The Lord be with all of you.

James 3:18 – A harvest of righteousness is sown in peace for those who make peace.

1 Peter 3:11 – Let them turn away from evil and do good; let them seek peace and pursue it.

WHAT TO DO

Be a peacemaker!

Build bridges!

Begin with surrender.

Consider this sentence: "The Beatitudes are a recipe for peace." How so? Whar are the ingredients for peace?

Consider: "With the Beatitudes you can begin to be a peacemaker even when you are mournful, or thirsty....even before you are complerely righteous!" Start building peace any time.

Let peace happen even before you are completely righteous and reconciled.

Consider: "Inner peace is the first effect of purity of heart." How?

Reflect on this sentence: "It's said that you can't be happy if you don't like yourself." Is this always true?

Reflect on the phrase of Studdert Kennedy's poem: ""Nothing but a great beginning!" How are we all "a great beginning"? What does that mean?

Think: How is this true? – "We can't really be right with ourselves, or with anyone else, for that matter, until we can be right with God."

Here's a heavy one: "God has reconciled all things to himself, making peace by the blood of the cross!" Think about that for a moment.

Break down more barriers! List a few.

"We need to cure the disease instead of merely salving the symptoms." How have we just salved the symptoms?

Think: What are "the seeds of conflict that might take root."

Make amends where needed.

A PRAYER

Almighty God, help me begin with surrender in my battle for peace. Give me grace to relinquish any barriers I uphold. Help me to see myself and others as children of God even before we have perfect peace. May wholeness and completeness be first in my mind as I consider the conflicts of life. Defeat my confusion with purity of heart, and help me make peace at every turn. In Jesus's name I pray. Amen.

A POEM

My Heart Is a Battlefield

My heart is a battlefield;
    The war's in my mind.
My faith is my strength and shield;
    But sin leaves me blind.

Collateral damage is seen when my love
    Becomes the first victim of all I believe.
And kindness is killed, when push comes to shove,
    And I even defend lies with the web that I weave.

I want to find peace, but I still want to win.
    And yet, I'm defeated. I've already lost.
I just can't imagine, yet, where to begin.
    I have destroyed and denied all the lines I have crossed.

    This battle must end, This conflict must cease.
    I have to surrender by fighting for peace.

CHAPTER EIGHT

THE PERSECUTED
PART ONE

Blessed are those who are persecuted for righteousness' sake,
for theirs is the kingdom of heaven.
Matthew 5:10

The Beatitudes – Blessed <u>are</u> the poor in spirit, the mournful, the meek, the-hungry-and-thirsty-for-righteousness. Blessed <u>are</u> the merciful, the pure in heart, the peacemakers. Blessed <u>are</u> those who are persecuted for righteousness' sake. The Beatitudes are a promise, and the promise is prophetic. Each Beatitude proclaims a present blessing and a future promise. But in prophecy, present and future cannot always be clearly distinguished.

On the surface it might seem as if the Beatitudes are looking for blessings in all the wrong places. Jesus did have a tendency to turn things upside down. Where the worldliness of the time seemed to claim the blessings of material abundance, Jesus proclaims the truer blessing of spiritual poverty. Where a worldliness seems to claim the blessings of a carefree lightheartedness, Jesus proclaims a truer blessing of mournful sorrow in the face of the world's shortcomings. Where worldliness claims the blessings of status and ambition, Jesus proclaims the truer blessing of a gentle meekness. Where worldliness claims the blessings of advancement and satisfaction no matter what the price, Jesus proclaims a truer blessing of a thirsty desire for righteousness.

And worldliness seems to ignore mercy, purity, and peacemaking completely, while Jesus proclaims them as divine virtues, relating us more closely with God. We are being freed from sin through our mercifulness, becoming visionary (seeing God) through our purity; and being called sons and daughters of God through our peacemaking,

And then Jesus brings this lesson full circle. Just as the poor in spirit are given the kingdom of heaven in the first beatitude, so likewise, do the righteous persecuted receive the kingdom of heaven. Only in those two is the promise in the present tense. In all others the promise is yet to come. But we must see each Beatitude as a kingdom promise, because the kingdom of God is not some future dream, but a present reality. The kingdom begins now, where Jesus is; and it began when Jesus came.

Blessing – The Beatitudes describe virtues, character traits we should all pursue, blessings. They are not just a formless ethical ideal, but a prescription for practical faith. They are not just principles to live by but flashes of righteous living piercing the darkness of the age. Yes, on the surface they seem to be searching for blessings in all the wrong places, but, look deeper, and you can see that the way of the Beatitudes is truly the way to happiness, to blessedness!

Happiness is like a window. Through it you can see heaven. And through the Beatitudes, Jesus is showing the way to heaven; to the place which he has prepared for us. And, in a world where so many other ways lead to destruction, Jesus shows the way to joy. And that blessedness begins now, the kingdom of heaven begins now, in the same way the feeling of being home begins with the first steps of the journey back. Theirs is the kingdom of heaven. And that happiness can be multiplied when it is divided. Share the joy that you're going home with someone once, and just watch them smile. Share the blessings you feel and they will bless others.

Those Persecuted for Righteousness' Sake – Let's stop and think for a moment. What happens when you try to share the blessings of being on the way to heaven? You might run into some rejection, you'll be called a religious fanatic. You might even be taunted, persecuted. You'll be told that you're so heavenly minded that you're no earthly good. But that will only happen if you forgo some of the other blessings of the Beatitudes, like meekness or peacemaking. Still Jesus tells us to expect a little persecution now and then. And if it happens the kingdom of heaven Is ours. People just won't understand what they can't imagine.

I can remember a missionary telling a congregation of people about trying to describe ice cream to a desert Bedouin. Not only was it impossible to get him to picture ice, but it was even difficult to talk about anything cold or frozen. You just can't teach someone the taste of something they've never imagined. And it's also true that you can no more talk about something you don't know then you can come back from where you've never been. That's why it's important to learn. And to learn we need to be students, disciples. The disciples were students of Jesus, learning about the true meaning of life. And Jesus told his disciples that they might and actually would be persecuted for what they knew. Not only persecuted, but reviled and slandered too. "They will utter all kinds of evil against you falsely... on my account." But he also told them to rejoice and to be glad, because it happened to the best of them. The prophets shared some pretty amazing insights; but because people either didn't want to be corrected, or, they couldn't conceive of the vision for themselves, they rejected the prophetic witness. And Jesus is the prime example of that. His goodness was not only a threat ro the status quo, but he preached about a kingdom that was to come, and, that was already here... His kingdom.

So, He was persecuted. How do you expect to be treated for being a disciple of Christ? Jesus said, in John 15:19, "Because you are not of the world, therefore, the world hates you." We are to be *in* the world but not *of* the world; we are to be transforming the world, not conforming to its ways. Jesus even said, "The hour is coming when whoever kills you will think they are offering service to God" (John 16:2).

It's difficult to be indifferent to a real, wide awake son or daughter of God! A whole body of sons and daughters of God confronts the community with a whole different way of life, a whole different set of values, a higher standard of righteousness. Christians confront the world with the kingdom of heaven <u>on earth.</u> The goodness and loving kindness of Christians are a threat to a worldly lifestyle, and, simply by the example of their righteousness, the Christian condemns without words the sins of the world in which they live, but of which they choose to rise above. Shine Your light in the eyes of a world in darkness and some will not like it; because truth is the enemy of pride; love is the enemy of selfishness; and faith is the enemy of false systems built on power and gratification. The blindness and cruelty of the ages have consistently rejected the truth even as the pharisees rejected Jesus.

Many times they tried to trap Him in order to prove to themselves that He was not true to the faith, and, to dissuade the people from accepting Him. Here's just a few examples:

> The Pharisees and Sadducees came up, and testing Jesus, they asked Him to show them a sign from heaven. But He replied to them, "When it is evening, you say, 'It will be fair weather, for the sky is red.' And in the morning, 'There will be a storm today, for the sky is red and threatening.' Do you know how to discern the appearance of the sky, but cannot discern the signs of the times?" (Matthew 16:1-4)

> He entered again into a synagogue; and a man was there whose hand was withered. They were watching Him to see if He would heal him on the Sabbath, so that they might accuse Him. (Mark 3:1-2)

> "The scribes and the Pharisees brought a woman caught in adultery, and having set her in the center of the court, they said to Him, 'Teacher, this woman has been caught in adultery, in the very act. Now in the law Moses commanded us to stone such women. Now what do you say?' They said this to test him, so that they might have some charge to bring against him" (John 8:3-6).

There are many other examples, but you get the idea that they rejected Jesus, and tried very hard to find fault. It is the sort of persecution we often see when people find fault with politicians and others in leadership. The Scriptures are full of the experiences of righteous people being persecuted.

The Psalms have many appeals to God for redeeming the faithful from persecution. Here's just one for now:

> Psalm 56:1-2 – Be gracious to me, O God, for people trample on me; all day long foes oppress me; my enemies trample on me all day long, for many fight against me. O Most High, when I am afraid, I put my trust in you.

Christian's organize their lives around Jesus as the central meaning to existence. The worldly put other things in the center. Christians are therefore naturally out of sync with the world. Christians "do not conform to this world but are transformed by the renewing of their minds, proving what is the will of God, what is good and acceptable and perfect" (Romans 12:2). By rejecting worldly standards of living, the early Christians seemed quite odd, especially in a world where a multitude of pagan gods were worshiped; in a world where subjects of the Roman Empire were required to worship the emperor.

For Righteousness' Sake – It is not a blessing just to be persecuted; but to be persecuted for righteousness' sake. It is not a blessing to be persecuted for preaching ourselves, for boasting; but we can always testify to what God is doing for us and through us. Paul even said,

> "What we preach is not ourselves but Jesus Christ as Lord and ourselves is your servants for Jesus' sake. For it is the God who said, 'Let light shine out of darkness,' who has shown in our hearts to give the light of the knowledge of the glory of God in the face of Christ. But we have this treasure in earthen vessels to show that the transcendent power belongs to God and not to us. We are afflicted in every way but not crushed; perplexed, but not driven to despair; persecuted, but not forsaken; struck down, but not destroyed; always carrying in the body the death of Jesus so that the life of Jesus may also be made manifest in our bodies. For while we live we are always being given up to death for Jesus's sake, so that the life of Jesus may be manifested in our mortal flesh" (2 Corinthians 4:5-11).

By rejecting worldly standards of living we have the treasure of the light of the knowledge of the glory of God shining in our hearts. We have this treasure in the earthen vessels of our bodies

A diamond is a piece of coal that made good under pressure. It comes from deep within the heart of the earth where it has been buried for millennia. But it seems to be a stone that is filled with light until the diamond is cut releasing the light. It seems to become more magnificent and precious as a prism, seeming to magnify and reflect outwardly more light than comes into it. God is within us like a diamond. Faith is a journey that discovers life and light. Faith is a process of mining inwardly in order to find that diamond of light within. Becoming a disciple is like becoming a diamond miner, learning that inward journey, and discovering what it is within us that truly reflects the light. By being light in a world of darkness, people who are used to the darkness will not stand for the brilliance of the truth we have to share. Still it is a blessing to be part of God's light!

<u>Theirs Is the Kingdom of Heaven</u> – The promise of this Beatitude is present tense, not future. It is the same promise given to the poor in spirit. The promise is the experience of heaven now!

First of all, if you are being persecuted for righteousness' sake, you must have hungered enough and thirsted enough for righteousness to be filled. That, in itself, is heaven! But consider what might have brought on the persecution. You were bold enough to defend and proclaim righteous living. You were willing to claim that righteousness is in Christ. There is a belief happening that is more than agreeing with doctrinal principles. True belief makes an investment. Those who might persecute you for your witness don't really have any more than a superficial belief; an easy belief. They accept Christ the way they might accept a mathematical equation. Math, however, doesn't save your soul.

You went out on a limb, took a risk, spoke up when righteousness was being slandered. You may even have attempted to persuade those persecuting you to see the light they needed so badly. You challenged them, their complacency, their worldly ways, their sin! You should be proud of your testimony. And they should have listened to you. There is respect due to those who fight for the Lord.

And there is honor. It is not earned by *thinking* about righteousness, but by walking with Christ in faith. In Romans 8:18, Paul says, "I consider that the sufferings of this present time are not worth comparing with the glory to be revealed in us." There's the posture needed by those who are persecuted for righteousness' sake. By virtue of our hope for glory, the Kingdom is promised, and, it is present even now. We are Kingdom people. We are already triumphant.

<u>The Journey Home</u> – Don't let a fear of persecution deter you from your journey. There will be difficult people along the way. But still, do God's will! We are on the road to triumph, inspite of the wickedness of those who would persecute us.

The Prodigal has felt defeat. He has turned his life, or, is turning his life around. He may be far from filled with righteousness, but he aches for it.

Part of me wants to embellish the story a bit. On his way home, he encounters helpless people and helps them. He encounters abusers bullying weakened people, and, he defends them. He has a new strength, now, that enables him not only to stand for what's right, but to do it, to prove what is right. Some of the people who have fought for justice so well are those who have experienced injustice more often than most.

Nothing inspires us to do what is right more than doing what is right, and, seeing results. Helping others and seeing them triumph. There is more to gain than we, with our limited imaginations can conceive. There is blessing... now!

Scriptures

To inspire a further consideration of an understanding of persecution, here are several relevant passages of Scripture:

Psalm 35:1 – Contend, O Lord, with those who contend with me. Fight against those who fight against me.

Psalm 39:8 – Deliver me from all my transgressions. do not make me the scorn of the fool.

Psalm 42:10-11 – As with a deadly wound in my body, my adversaries taunt me, while they say to me continually, "Where is your God?" Why are you cast down, O my soul, and why are you disquieted within me? Hope in God; for I shall again praise him, my help and my God.

Psalm 43:1 – Vindicate me, O God, and defend my cause against an ungodly people; from those who are deceitful and unjust deliver me.

Psalm 55:1-3 – Give ear to my prayer, O God; do not hide yourself from my supplication. Attend to me, and answer me; I am troubled in my complaint. I am distraught by the noise of the enemy, because of the clamor of the wicked. For they bring trouble upon me, and in anger they cherish enmity against me.

Psalm 59:1-2– Deliver me from my enemies, O my God; protect me from those who rise up against me. Deliver Me from those who work evil; from the bloodthirsty save me.

Psalm 143:9 – Save Me, O Lord, from my enemies; I have fled to you for refuge.

Matthew 5:44b – Love your enemies and pray for those who persecute you.

Matthew 10:16-18 – Behold, I am sending you out like sheep into the midst of wolves; so be wise as serpents and innocent as doves. Beware of them, for they will hand you over to councils and flog you in their synagogues; and you will be dragged before governors and kings because of me, as a testimony to them and the Gentiles.

Matthew 10:22 – You will be hated by all because of my name. But the one who endures to the end will be saved.

John 16:33b – In the world you face persecution. But take courage; I have overcome the world!

Acts 14:22 – It is through many persecutions that we must enter the kingdom of God.

Romans 8:18 – I consider that the sufferings of this present time are not worth comparing with the glory about to be revealed to us.

Romans 8:35-37 – Who will separate us from the love of Christ? Will hardship, or distress, or persecution, or famine, or nakedness, or peril, or sword? As it is written, "For your sake we are being killed all day long; we are counted as sheep to be slaughtered." No, in all these things we are more than conquerors through him who loved us.

1 Corinthians 4:12c – When persecuted, we endure.

2 Corinthians 4:8-9 – We are afflicted in every way, but not crushed; perplexed, but not driven to despair; persecuted, but not forsaken; struck down, but not destroyed.

2 Corinthians 12:9-10 – So I will boast all the more gladly of my weaknesses, so that the power of Christ may dwell in me. Therefore I am content with weaknesses, insults, hardships, persecutions, and calamities for the sake of Christ; for whenever I am weak then I am strong.

2 Timothy 3:10-12 – Now you have observed my teaching, my conduct, my aim in life, my faith, my patience, my love, my steadfastness, my persecutions, and my suffering the things that happened to me in Antioch, Iconium, and Lystra. What persecutions I endured! Yet the Lord rescued me from all of them. Indeed all who want to live a Godly life in Christ Jesus will be persecuted.

1 Peter 4:12 – Beloved do not be surprised at the fiery ordeal that is taking place among you to test you, as though something strange were happening to you.

James 1:2-3 – My brothers and sisters, whenever you face trials of any kind, consider it nothing but joy, because you know that the testing of your faith produces endurance.

What to Do

Compare the Beatitudes with the ways of the world. Do they always disagree?

Think: If Jesus Christ is King, where is His Kingdom?

Share your blessings, and you will bless others.

Consider: "People just won't understand what they can't imagine." How can we help people imagine being blessed, finding heaven…?

Be a disciple, a student. Learn.

Answer this question: How do you expect to be treated for being a disciple of Christ?

Consider this sentence: "Shine Your light in the eyes of a world in darkness and some will not like it." How have you experienced this?

"Do not conform to this world but be transformed by the renewing of your minds, proving what is the will of God, what is good and acceptable and perfect" (Romans 12:2).

Be bold enough to defend and proclaim righteous living.

Take the risk. Speak up. Challenge people who seem to love the darkness.

Don't let a fear of persecution deter you from your journey.

Love your enemies and pray for those who persecute you.

Consider that the sufferings of this present time are not worth comparing with the glory about to be revealed to us.

Make God your shelter!

A Prayer

Almighty God, there are always difficult people to be met in our life's journeys; help us to keep the hope of your blessings vital in our hearts and minds. When we are persecuted, when people stand against us, when we are treated unfairly, help us to be content, and help us to contend for Your ways and Your righteous Kingdom. Give us peace, and help us make peace with our enemies by loving them, by showing them light, and by standing with You. This we pray in Jesus' name. Amen.

A Poem

You're So Used to the Darkness

You're so used to the darkness
    That you can't stand the light.
And then you're resentful
    When the dawn is too bright.

    You hate me for trying
        To help you to see
    But I know that it's true
        That the truth sets you free

I know you keep squinting,
    You cover your eyes.
You keep turning away,
    Believing in lies.

You like all the shadows,
    You persecute me.
But I stand for the vision –
    Let righteousness be.

    You hate me for trying
        To help you to see
    But I know that it's true
        That the truth sets you free

CHAPTER NINE

THE PERSECUTED.
PART TWO,
REJOICE!

Blessed are you when people revile you
and persecute you
and utter all kinds of evil against you falsely
on my account.
Rejoice and be glad,
for your reward is great in heaven,
for in the same way
they persecuted the prophets who were before you.
Matthew 5:11-12

The Beatitudes – Many people adopt a "Code of Ethics" for their lives. Such a code can create boundaries for behavior, but they also create a pattern for life. The Golden Rule is to "Do unto others as you would like others to do unto you" (Matthew 7:12) I have known many people who have vowed to do their best to create a better world, or, environment, for their children and for generations yet to come.

The Beatitudes are a "code of ethics". Honesty, integrity, hope, and dreams (among other things) can all figure in to what we might claim as a code of ethics. Philosophers and historians have worked hard, sometimes, to discern a code of ethics for people to follow. Based on the values considered most relevant, such a "code" can apply selectively to a business, a sports team, a social club, a family, or any group or individual.

The hard part comes when individuals dichotomize their behavior – this for my business, and that for my friends, etc. Some people have no code of ethics other than what is motivated by self-interest. It is hard to live in a community, and, get along, if there is no code of ethics. And, with the Beatitudes, Jesus is setting forward His Code of Ethics. The ethics of His Kingdom. As a disciple of Christ, I accept His Code of Ethics.

Blessing – When Jesus began to preach, His initial message was, "Repent, for the Kingdom of Heaven is at hand!" (Matthew 4:17). Then, "As he walked by the Sea of Galilee, he saw two brothers, Simon who is called Peter, and Andrew, his brother, casting a net into the sea; for they were fishermen. And he said to them, 'Follow me, and I will make you fishers of men.' Immediately, they left their nets and followed him. Going on from there he saw two other brothers, James, the son of Zebedee, and John, his brother, in the boat with their father, mending their nets, and he called them. Immediately, they left the boat and their father, and followed him" (Matthew 4:18-22).

What might it mean to follow Jesus immediately? In a way, It expresses a sense of urgency. In Luke, Jesus says, "If anyone comes to me and does not hate his own father and mother and wife and children and brothers and sisters, yes, and even his own life, they cannot be my disciple" (Luke 14:26).

Now, I don't believe that the Prince of Peace really means that to be his disciples, we must alienate ourselves from our families. No. Jesus wants us to be peacemakers. He is teaching by speaking in extremes, the way a parent might warn a child when they are playing near the street to be careful, "because they might get run over by a truck." That image is very extreme, because the child might only get hit by a car!

Jesus is saying what he does, because he cannot impress upon the people enough, the importance and urgency of being disciples. And so he also says, "Whoever does not bear his own cross and come after, me cannot be my disciple" (Luke 14:27). Jesus even went so far at one point to suggest "selling all that you have and distribute it to the poor and you will have treasure in heaven, and come, follow me" (Luke 18:22).

Jesus knew that whenever our loyalties of faith intersected with the pressures of the worldliness in out midst, there was a cross the bear. And at every such intersection, there's a cross for the disciples of Jesus.

But the cross is a blessing. Yes, it is a symbol of sacrifice, but it is also the means of forgiveness, reconciliation, atonement, and love. Disciples of Jesus accept this blessing. The urgency, the immediacy of following Jesus, reveals its importance. The disciples became disciples even before Jesus taught them. They did not wait until they understood everything before they linked their lives to the life of Christ. They linked their lives to him and *then* he taught them. If you wait to understand the faith completely before you are faithful, you will never be faithful. Trust and belief are followed by commitment, and commitment is followed by understanding; but it is also true that commitment can be followed by trust and belief, and then comes understanding. And many people want understanding before they will trust, believe, or commit. I have compared it with driving: You don't need to understand the internal combustion engine, before you get into a car. However it comes, there's something important here. The blessing is important. It is a natural part of faith, discipleship.

When People Revile You and Persecute You — I've said it many times in different ways: we treat others with love not because of who they are, but because of who *we* are. We treat others with kindness not because they have earned it, but because we are kind. We treat others with blessing not because they deserve a blessing, but because we are blessed and we can share it.

Being a Christian is no piece of cake. It is not an easy life. There are bad times for Christians just as there are bad times for non-christians. But Christians maintain a unique perspective about things. Peter, in his First Letter, asked, "What credit is it if when you do wrong and are beaten for it, you take it patiently? But if, when you do right and suffer for it, you take it patiently; you have God's approval" (1 Peter 2:20) Blessing! And James said, in his Letter, "Count it all joy, my brothers and sisters, when you meet various trials. For you know that the testing of your faith produces steadfastness. And let steadfastness have its full effect, that you may be perfect and complete, lacking in nothing" (James 1:2-4). And then, of steadfastness, he says. "If any of you lacks wisdom, let them ask God, who gives to all generously without reproaching, and it will be given to them. But let them ask in faith, with no doubting, for they who doubt are like a wave of the sea that is driven and tossed by the wind. For that person must not suppose that a double-minded person, unstable in all their ways, will receive anything from the Lord. (James 1:5-8).

A double-minded person!? With what inner struggles do you wrestle? What are the dilemmas you face in your life? There's an inward persecution I feel when I experience the guilt of being a back-sliding sinner; there's an inward persecution I feel when I act unlovingly and feel shame; and when I put other things before God and feel anxious; and when I think of my unworthiness, and fear God's judgment upon me. But I'm also persecuted by the hurt I feel for the hungry, by the sadness I feel for the neglected and abused, by the loss I feel for those who are perishing for lack of faith; for the darkness in which so many people live. "We are afflicted in every way, but not crushed; perplexed, but not driven to despair; persecuted, but not forsaken; struck down, but not destroyed (2 Corinthians 4:8 9). \We need to keep perspective. Claim triumph, not defeat.

Perspective! "I say to you, do not resist one who is evil. But if anyone strikes you in the right cheek, turn to them the other also; and if anyone would sue you and take your coat, let them have your cloak as well; and if anyone forces you to go one mile go with them two miles." "Love your enemies, and pray for those who persecute you, so that y,ou may be sons and daughters of your Father who is in heaven" (Matthew 5:39-41 and 44-45).

Blessed are you when others revile you and persecute you and utter all kinds of evil against you falsely on my account. You're not blessed just because you're persecuted. There are a lot of people who go around saying, "Look at me, I'm persecuted, I'm being rejected, so I must be right!" Just ask them if they're being rejected on Christ's account, or if they feel like they're being persecuted for righteousness' sake? We need to help each other keep perspective.

Your Reward Is Great in Heaven – In heaven! The reward cannot be measured in human terms it's ours now. "Your reward is great!" But it's in heaven. That means that all the more will Christ prepare a place for you. But remember, a Christian that seems uncommitted, or too compromising. or double-minded will never be persecuted on Christ's account. And in some areas of the world, where Christianity seems to be a very serious threat to the status quo, today, Christians are persecuted. They're rejected and afflicted just for being Christians. In our society, today, Christians aren't really persecuted, they're ignored.

In our culture, Christians aren't really that different from the rest of the people. Christians don't cause much of a threat anymore. Part of the reason is because our society is partly based on religious tolerance. Another part of the reason is that Christians today don't stand up for their beliefs the way they ought to. "Blessed are those who are persecuted for righteousness sake for theirs is the kingdom of heaven."

Persecution comes in many forms. There's the outward violence, the slander of words; and then, there's the inward distress brought on by personal self-persecution due to confusion and self-confrontation. But what about a confrontation of a different kind: Peer pressure. Peer pressure can be a powerful persecutor. Young people are often led into the abuse of alcohol and drugs, and, immoral conduct under the fear of the persecuting taunts from classmates and the people they want to call their friends. Insults and put-downs are the kind of persecution that tends to attack a person's self-esteem in such a way that it can be devastating. It's no wonder people so often go along with the crowd.

I can remember being laughed at by the hippie crowd because I was a straight jock in high school. I was called a chicken because I refused to do some dope with people who had at one time been my friends. And then, on the other hand, I can remember Peter being pushed around because he was a brain and he wasn't athletic. He was taunted, and it hurt him; so I defended him. I told his taunters that the world is run by the smart people not by the people who think they're tough. Back in 1982, I was serving in my first appointment in Brookville, Illinois, where there was a girl in the junior class at Lanark High School who became so depressed from insults and put-downs about her weight, that she came home one day after school and committed suicide.

The pressure gets to us. But faith can help. We need to be able to say,

"The Lord is my light and my salvation. Whom shall I fear? The Lord is the stronghold of my life; of whom shall I be afraid? When evil doers assail me, uttering slanders against me, my adversaries and foes – they shall stumble and fall. Though a host encamp against me, my heart shall not fear. Though war rise against me yet I will be confident. One thing have I asked of the Lord, that will

I seek after; that I may dwell in the house of the Lord all the days of my life, to behold the beauty of the Lord, and to inquire in his Temple. For he will hide me in his shelter in the day of trouble; he will conceal me under the cover of his tent; he will set me high upon a rock" (Psalm 27:1-5).

In spite of the pressure of persecuting taunts you can choose to be happy anyway. Some people are happy or unhappy by choice. If you start with a positive attitude, you can withstand anything. In Zechariah 9:12, we're told, "Return to your stronghold, O prisoners of hope; today I declare that I will restore to you double." We must be like prisoners of hope, believing in the sun even when it's not shining. If you love life, life will love you back! Realize that you are free to choose how you will react to what happens to you. When something destructive, or, counter-productive is happening, we need to choose wisely the meanings we give to those occasions. When I was ridiculed in college because I was a churchgoer, it was not I who was wrong, it was not the church that was wrong, it was the attitude that my supposed friends had that was wrong. By being positive, we can choose our perspective in any situation. We can't just sit and say "if only…" "If only they had been raised to enjoy the Bible… If only they had been taught to see the Bible as a powerful resource for the spirit… if only…" Instead, we need to say, "Next time…" Next time, things are going to be different. Next time… for now rejoice.

In the same way they persecuted the profits who were before you – There has always been persecution. It happened to the best. It happened to Jesus. Why? Partly because the truth about human nature is somewhat too revealing. We don't like it when we are called to be accountable to the best standards of our culture, nor especially, to the higher standards of the faith. We don't like being exposed. I liked what George W. Bush said, as our President, the day after 9/11/2001. He called out followers of Islam and said, "That's not what Islam is about." He said, "**The face of terror is not the true faith of Islam**. That's not what Islam is all about. Islam is peace. These terrorists don't represent peace."

The standards of the terrorists changed the world in many ways, …for a while. What the terrorists of 9/11 did to Islam brought more shame on Muslims than hope. We all, likewise need to claim the truth of what we stand for, even in the face of persecution.

<u>The Journey Home</u> – I don't know how long his journey might have been, but the Prodigal *had* gone into "a far country". So, I imagine at least several days, if not a few weeks on foot. Did he travel alone? Would anyone have joined him, fresh from the pigstyes? Did he travel at night? He was "on the run" in some ways. Did he want to go unnoticed?

He has escaped a life he never thought he'd live, and is returning to the refuge of his father's home. Nowhere to go, accept home! This is the way we should see our journeys. This is the way we should think about God, hoping God will "take us in."

By now, the prodigal is close. The landscapes are familiar. The villages near his father's home are the same. Might somebody recognize him? No. He looks different, somehow. His clothes are probably filthy… unless he procured some spare clothes somewhere along the way. He might smell filthy… unless he bathed in a stream he passed. Does he have a bit of a limp from all the walking he's done?

I imagine he is trembling. He is weak from the road. Has he eaten much? When was his last meal? He is nervous about seeing his old home, his father, his older brother. Will he be rejected? Or will there be something sweet about the reunion. He has probably played it out a thousand times as he traveled. He has rehearsed his reconciliation speech. He knows he can't expect much because he has dishonored his father so deeply. "Just let me be one of your slaves." He believes that being a slave in his father's house is better than anything else anywhere else.

But he has hope. He hopes for a minimal amount of grace. It feels good even to think of the minimum. He feels blessed already. The time has come. Will his father even be home?

Scriptures

To inspire a further consideration of an understanding of reasons to rejoice, here are several relevant passages of Scripture:

Deuteronomy 16:11 – Rejoice before the Lord your God – you and your sons and your daughters, your male and female slaves, the Levites resident in your towns, as well as the strangers, the orphans, and the widows who are among you – at the place that the Lord your God will choose as a dwelling for his name.

1 Samuel 11:15 – So all the people went to Gilgal, and there they made Saul King before the Lord in Gilgal. There they sacrificed offerings of well-being before the Lord, and there Saul and all the Israelites rejoiced greatly.

Psalm 5:11 – Let all who take refuge in you rejoice; let them ever sing for joy. Spread your protection over them, so that those who love your name may exult in you.

Psalm 32:11 – Be glad in the Lord and rejoice, O righteous, and shout for joy, all you upright in heart.

Psalm 64:10 – Let the righteous rejoice in the Lord and take refuge in him. Let all the upright in heart Glory.

Psalm 97:11-12 – Light dawns for the righteous, and joy for the upright in heart. Rejoice in the Lord, O you righteous, and give thanks to His holy name!

Psalm 100:1 – I will sing of loyalty and of justice; to you, O Lord, I will sing.

Isaiah 29:19 – The meek shall obtain fresh joy in the Lord, and the neediest people shall exalt in the Holy One of Israel.

Zechariah 9:9 – Rejoice greatly, O daughter Zion! Shout aloud, O daughter Jerusalem Lo, your king comes to you, triumphant and victorious is he, humble and riding on a donkey, on a colt, the foal of a donkey.

Matthew 2:10 – When they saw that the star had stopped, they were overwhelmed with joy.

Luke 1:46-47 – And Mary said, "My soul magnifies the Lord, and my spirit rejoices in God my savior."

Luke 10:20 – "Nevertheless, do not rejoice at this, that the spirits submit to you, but rejoice that your names are written in heaven."

Luke 15:10 – "Just so, I tell you, there is joy in the presence of the angels of God over one sinner who repents."

John 16:24 – "Ask and you will receive, so that your joy may be complete.".

Acts 5:41 – As they left the council, they rejoiced that they were considered worthy to suffer dishonor for the sake of the name.

Romans 12:15 – Rejoice with those who rejoice.

Romans 15:13 – May the God of hope fill you with all joy and peace in believing, so that you may abound in hope by the power of the Holy Spirit.

1 Corinthians 13:6 – Love does not rejoice in wrongdoing but rejoices in the truth.

2 Corinthians 6:8b-10 – We are treated as Impostors, and yet are true; as unknown and yet are well known; as dying, and see – we are alive; as punished, and yet not killed; as sorrowful, yet always rejoicing; as poor, yet making many rich; as having nothing, yet possessing everything..

Philippians 4:4 – Rejoice in the lord always, again I will say, Rejoice.

1 Thessalonians 5:16 – Rejoice always.

1 Peter 1:8 – Although you have not seen him, you love him; and even though you do not see him now, you believe in him and rejoice with an Indescribable and glorious joy.

What to Do

Obviously: Rejoice!

Develop a "code of ethics" for yourself. Or, accept what the Scriptures claim as such a code.

Feel a sense of urgency about following Jesus.

Consider some of the ways people sometimes teach by speaking in extremes.

Consider what it might mean to bear your own cross.

Consider this sentence: "The disciples became disciples even before Jesus taught them." What is the point?

Think about this statement: "We treat others with blessing not because they deserve a blessing, but because we are blessed and we can share it." How is this true?

Don't be "double-minded." Remember purity of heart.

Claim triumph, not defeat!

Help others keep the right perspective.

Think: How has peer-pressure been a persecutor in your life?

Be like a prisoner of hope, believing in the sun even when it's not shining.

Claim the truth of what we stand for!

Take refuge in God.

A Prayer

O almighty God, You are our refuge and our comfort; You are our hope and our confidence. We trust you to carry us through the ordeals of this life, and, that Christ is preparing a place for us in His Father's house. Give us grace to know that Your light is shining even when the darkness of this world makes it difficult to see. And help us in our journeys, for the way is hard, and we are weak. This we pray in Jesus' name. Amen.

A Song

I Will Choose to Rejoice

Hate me for the light I carry.
    Hate me for the truth I know
Lie about me like I'm scary.
    Tell me where you think I'll go.

Don't believe a word I'm saying
    Don't give me the time of day.
Laugh at me when I am praying
    Act as if I've lost my way.

    But I still know I have a choice
    And I will choose to rejoice.

Everything I say is disputed
    All I to do is always "wrong."
Even though I'm persecuted
    I will sing a faithful song

I can see the sunlight shining.
    Darkness has a hold on you.
I will tolerate your whining.
    I'll keep saying what is true.

    As long as I still have a voice
    I will choose to rejoice

CONCLUSION: COMING HOME

COMING HOME

While he was still far off,
his father saw him
and was filled with compassion;
he ran and put his arms around him and kissed him.
Then the son said to him,
"Father, I have sinned
against heaven and before you.
I am no longer worthy to be called your son."
But the father said to his slaves,
"Quickly, bring out a robe – the best one – and put it on him;
put a ring on his finger and sandals on his feet.
And get the fatted calf and kill it,
and let us eat and celebrate;
for this son of mine was dead and is alive again;
he was lost and is found!"
And they began to celebrate.
Luke 15:20b-24

<u>Arriving Home</u> – Not only was his father home, but he was looking down the lane! How had *his* stay-at-home journey given him hope? What had he been thinking? He said it was like his son was dead; it was like his son was lost. How was he feeling while his younger son was away? Did he focus more on his older son? Did they wonder about him? Or was he considered a "lost cause"?

I think it's important to hear Christ's word "compassion" used to describe the father in the story. The father was "filled with compassion". The story contrasts the father's compassion with the older son's wall of resentment and bitterness toward his prodigal brother. What did the father know of his older son's attitude? Often we impose our own notions into the story. We retell it from different perspectives, sometimes, in order to give the story greater depth, and to proclaim certain lessons. For example, how did the older brother "know" about his younger brother's activities, like, how he had "devoured your property with prostitutes" ? (Luke 15:30).

One thing to consider is how most parents don't just think of the present circumstances in their children's lives. When I think of my son or daughter, I picture them in my arms as babies, taking their first steps, going to school, learning, learning, learning, growing. Their accomplishments flash into my mind from various stages of their lives. There is pride and hope, and worry that is remembered. It is seldom just one memory, but hundreds that flood my mind. Did the father in this story think that way? How could he not? He felt as though "this son of mine was dead... lost" (Luke 15:24). When someone you have loved seems "gone", you can't help but think of them often (all the time?). You imagine how things would be different if they were still "here".

Consider that compassion of the father. I think we are supposed to see God's love and mercy in the story. I am touched by the hymn, "How Deep the Father's Love for Us". I could imagine it being used afer a sermon about the prodigal father:

> How deep the Father's love for us,
>> How vast beyond all measure
> That He should give His only Son
>> To make a wretch His treasure.

The love, compassion, and mercy of the father is magnified by the gift we have of Christ's crucifixion, death, and resurrection. The prodigal son had become a "wretch", but was still loved. He had obviously lost his way, but he's "here" again. The prodigal wanted to change his "here". He believed that the lowest place in his father's house would be much, much better than his circumstances when he hit bottom, "when he came to himself" (Luke 15:17).

The "welcome home" of the father brings tears to my eyes. The prodigal doesn't even get to give his whole remorseful speech. The father almost cuts him off with the orders to his servants to bring a fine robe, sandals, and a ring for his "lost" son's finger. They were going to celebrate with a feast! It was not because the father was proud, but because he was just so glad to see his son...alive.

And although the older brother resists and complains, the way I want the story to end is that he eventually comes around to his father's attitude, and welcomes his brother. I believe in the blessing.

The Beatitudes – That's what The Beatitudes are all about! Blessing! They are a "system" for blessing. Now, if you don't like the idea of being coerced into a "system" of some kind, let me just ask if you use a clock, or, a calendar? They are systems for telling time. Do you use the system of mathematics? Why not a system for faith, for hope, for blessing? I know it's not the same. Faith and blessings are more subjective. They depend on you, the subject, applying the "system". We're not all the same when it comes to the Beatitudes, the way we are all the same before the calendar. But... we all want to be happy. It's a natural inclination built into human nature.

The Beatitudes pronounce a blessing on almost every aspect of life. And though we might not choose to be "poor in Spirit", or, "meek', or "persecuted", there are special blessings to be discovered when we go through those difficulties. The promises of the Beatitudes draw us forward. There may be what we might call "negative" aspects of the Beatitudes, but even when we are lost, we can discover things; even when we are mournful, we can appreciate our surroundings, enjoy the scenery, realize good times are still ahead.

Our expectations may change a bit. The Prodigal lowered his. But he believed in something better than his current situation.

Blessing – Something better. Imagine having a wound on your right foot. You try to stay off it and you walk very carefully... with a limp. You might even "baby" yourself a bit. Now imagine that wound healing after a long time. Your gait becomes normal again. You don't feel like it is risky to walk any more. The imagined wellness gives you something to look forward to. Hope. The blessings we have known tell us that there are blessings yet to come. The vision of a better day is a blessing even in our worst moments. That is what a blessing can be.

You would never tell a crying child about something sadder. You want to cheer them up. Jesus is doing this by teaching the Beatitudes. Be a cheerleader in someone's life. Give hope. Proclaim a blessedness for the future. Even when the football team is losing badly, the cheerleaders still dance. They express hope, and, they shake their pompoms. They still say "Yea!" Faith can enable such a posture. Belief can give hope and strength. Yes, we can still be weak, but the future is strong!

Come to Me – Jesus proclaims a blessing to those who come to Him: "Come to me, all you that are weary and are carrying heavy burdens, and I will give you rest. Take my yoke upon you, and learn from me; for I am gentle and humble in heart, and you will find rest for your souls. For my yoke is easy, and my burden is light" (Matthew 11:28-30). He doesn't use the word "blessed" but he promises "rest".

When we come to Christ we discover as much about ourselves as we do about Him. His word may make us aware of the poverty in our lives. We will grieve our brokenness. It will make us meeker, and we will discover our true hunger. Our need for mercy will make us merciful; and purer hearts will bring us visions. When that vision begins to include peace, we will begin to find rest. And in spite of resistance and persecution, we will be able to focus more and more on our ultimate goal – heaven.

The reward for the journey is compassion, abundant grace, and eternal rest. I am blessed! You are blessed. We are a blessing to others!

Scripture

To inspire a further consideration of eternal rest, here are several relevant passages of Scripture:

Genesis 2:3 – So God blessed the seventh day and hallowed it, because on it God rested from all the work he had done in creation.

Exodus 33:14 – He said, "My presence will go with you and I will give you rest."

Psalm 4:8 – I will both lie down and sleep in peace; for you alone, O Lord, make Me lie down and safety.

Psalm 23 – The Lord is my shepherd, I shall not want. He makes me lie down in green pastures; he leads me besides still waters; he restores my soul. He leads me in the paths of righteousness for his name's sake. Even though I walk through the darkest valley, I fear no evil; for you are with me; your rod and your staff – they comfort me. You prepare a table before me in the presence of my enemies; you anoint my head with oil; my cup overflows. Surely goodness and mercy shall follow me all the days of my life, and I will dwell in the house of the Lord my whole life long.

Psalm 46:10 – Be still, and know that I am God! I am exalted among the nations, I am exalted in the Earth.

Psalm 55:6 – And I say, O that I had wings like a dove! I would fly away and be at rest.

Proverbs 19:23 – The fear of the Lord is life indeed; filled with it one rests secure and suffers no harm.

Isaiah 26:3 – Those of steadfast mind you keep in peace – in peace because they trust in you.

Isaiah 30:15 – In returning and rest you shall be saved; in quietness and in trust shall be your strength.

Isaiah 40:31 – Those who wait upon the Lord shall renew their strength, they shall mount up with wings like eagles, they shall run and not be weary, they shall walk and not faint.

Isaiah 48:22 – "There is no peace," says the Lord, "for the wicked."

Isaiah 57:2 – And they enter into peace; those who walk uprightly will rest on their couches.

Mark 6:31 – He said to them, "Come away to a deserted place all by yourselves and rest a while."

John 14:27 – "Peace I leave with you; my peace I give to you. I do not give to you as the world gives. Do not let your hearts be troubled, and do not let them be afraid."

Philippians 4:6-7 – Do not worry about anything, but in everything by prayer and supplication with thanksgiving, let your requests be made known to God. And the peace of God, which surpasses all understanding, will guard your hearts and your minds in Christ Jesus.

Hebrews 4:9-11 – So then, a sabbath rest still remains for the people of God; for those who enter God's rest also cease from their labors as God did from his. Let us therefore make every effort to enter that rest, so that no one may fall through such disobediences as theirs.

What to Do

Never think of anyone as a "lost cause".

Be compassionate. Have mercy.

Don't just think of the present circumstances in someone's life.

Imagine how things would be different if someone "gone" was "here" again.

See God's love and mercy in the story of The Prodigal Son.

See the Beatitudes as a "system" for blessing.

Realize there are special blessings to be discovered when we go through our difficulties.

Believe in something better than your current situation.

Believe that the blessings we have known tell us that there are blessings yet to come.

Be a cheerleader in someone's life.

Believe that the future is strong!

Come to Christ, and you will find rest!

Let the peace of God, which surpasses all understanding, guard your hearts and your minds in Christ Jesus.

A Prayer

Almighty God, my shelter, my rest, and my peace, help me in my journey home. It seems like I have so far to go, and the way is hard. Be with me, please. You have set my feet on this path, and I believe I can find mercy at its end. Give me hope again and again, for I sometimes feel hopeless. I no longer feel lost because I have the right directions. May every milestone I pass remind me that the past is behind me, and my future is filled with light. This I pray in Jesus' name. Amen.

A Poem

Home at Last

It feels as if the darkness is gone
    Whenever I keep my eyes on the light.
I believe there's a wonderful, colorful dawn
    Forged by the starshine of every long night.

The sun keeps on rising over my heart
    Over the edge of life so far away;
And I keep on waking with every new start
    Of every new morning, every new day.

The world has a way of telling us all
    To just carry on by renewing your mind;
Trusting the promise, the purpose, the call,
    The vision, the joy, and the hope we can find.

    With every step forward, the pain of the past
    Seems further behind me, and I'll be home at last!

THE END AGAIN

Printed in the United States
by Baker & Taylor Publisher Services